INTRODUCTION TO

ADVOCACY

RESEARCH, WRITING, AND ARGUMENT

Sixth Edition

Edited by
Heather Leal
Syrena Case
Barbara Fiacco
Joe Gershman
Marc Goldstein
Dana Kirchman
Kim Stallings

Board of Student Advisers
Harvard Law School
Cambridge, Massachusetts

Westbury, New York
THE FOUNDATION PRESS, INC.
1996

Library of Congress Cataloging-in-Publication Data
Introduction to advocacy : research, writing, and arguments / prepared
 by Board of Student Advisers, Harvard Law School, Cambridge,
 Massachusetts. — 6th ed.
       p.   cm.
   Includes index.
   ISBN 1–56662–351–0 (soft cover)
   1. Moot courts.   2. Briefs--United States.   3. Legal composition.
   4. Legal research—United States.   I. Harvard Law School.   Board of
   Student Advisers.
 KF281.A2I57   1996
 808'.066347—dc20   96–8774

Cover artwork:
James Casebere
COURTROOM, 1979–80
duratan on lightbox, 40" x 50"
Art and the Law 1988
Copyright 1988 West Publishing
Eagan, MN

 PRINTED ON 10% POST CONSUMER RECYCLED PAPER

PREFACE

Most first-year law students are required to take a course in legal research, writing, and oral advocacy, or to participate in a moot court program. Of the many interesting courses you will have during your years in law school, your lawyering course will be among the most useful. Learning to be an effective advocate takes time and practice, but law schools recognize that an introduction to the basic skills is an important component of every lawyer's education. An introductory lawyering course may be the only opportunity you have to translate your classroom learning into practical work before you take your first legal job.

This book focuses exclusively on the litigation model of dispute resolution, because that is the model emphasized in many first-year courses. However, the emphasis on litigation belies its importance in American legal practice. Much of what is thought of as litigation settles before either party ever appears in court; lawyers spend a substantial amount of time advising clients, rather than prosecuting or defending cases; and negotiation and mediation are fast becoming preferred means of resolving disputes. Nonetheless, every lawyer is well-served by a solid foundation in written and oral advocacy skills.

To help you sort through the legal problems presented in your lawyering course, this book analyzes the various stages of work you will do to reach resolutions. It begins with the moment when you first learn the factual context of a potential case and ends with oral argument, after you have researched and analyzed possible claims and defenses, as well as briefed the most persuasive arguments for your side. Examples in every chapter are drawn from *Bell-Wesley v. O'Toole*, a hypothetical wrongful pregnancy action brought by the parents of an unplanned child against the doctor who negligently performed the father's vasectomy. The full record, a legal research memorandum, and appellate briefs for both sides appear in Appendices B, D, and E.

Each chapter is designed to be self-contained. If your task were to prepare a legal research memorandum on the strengths of possible claims, you could read this book through Chapter 3, "Writing a Legal Research Memorandum." Furthermore, many issues are briefed, but never argued orally, because of judicial time constraints. Thus, on a motion for summary judgment, you might have to provide a memorandum of points and authorities opposing the motion (a "brief") for the court, but would not necessarily need to prepare for oral argument. In that case, you could profitably review the chapters on facts, research, and brief writing, without

concerning yourself with other topics. You should view this book as a resource to accompany you as you become familiar with legal advocacy; adapt it to fit your individual style and needs.

One final and very important point is that you will need to make strategic and stylistic choices throughout the process of handling a given legal problem. The art of advocacy is necessarily a product of your own tastes and personality. There is no "right" way to research an issue, write a memorandum, or draft a brief. This book offers you alternatives wherever possible; you should choose among them at will. Any attempt at prescription would be foolhardy; take advantage of the many colors on your palette.

PREFACE TO THE SIXTH EDITION

The sixth edition of *Introduction to Advocacy* expands on and updates the legal research, brief writing, and oral argument techniques presented in the first five editions. However, it departs from previous editions in philosophy and approach. The sixth edition is designed to be an effective companion for any introductory lawyering course taught from a litigation perspective. Although the fictional legal problem used to exemplify the basic concepts is set in the appellate context, the sixth edition no longer focuses on moot court to the exclusion of other exercises. To this end, the "Reading the Record" chapter has been replaced by an "Interpreting Facts and Developing Core Theory" chapter, which emphasizes understanding facts in context and developing a coherent core theory of a case. Beyond teaching digestion of facts, the chapter leads students through a process of discovering the malleability of facts, storytelling in legal writing, and integrating factual interpretations into core theory.

Additionally, the sixth edition includes a new chapter entitled "Writing a Legal Research Memorandum." This chapter discusses memorandum structure, purpose, and writing style. It suggests ways of beginning the writing process and of identifying the precise legal issues to be addressed. It contrasts the legal research memorandum with the brief, illustrating the functional and stylistic differences between these two types of legal documents. Included in Appendix D is a new sample legal research memorandum which was written as background for the appellant's sample brief in Appendix E.

Each chapter has been substantially revised to reflect current trends in legal research, writing, and argument. In particular, the "Legal Research" chapter suggests ways of fruitfully integrating computer and book research; "Writing a Brief" explains the importance of standard of review to the appellate brief writer; and "Oral Argument" considers methods of public speaking in improving communication during oral argument. The "General Rules of Style and Citation of Authorities" appendix has been revised to conform to rules promulgated in the sixteenth edition of *The Bluebook*, published by the Harvard Law Review Association. Most rules are illustrated with textual examples and referenced to the corresponding *Bluebook* rules to facilitate learning of that professional guide.

ACKNOWLEDGMENT

Introduction to Advocacy originally appeared as a pamphlet to guide first-year students through the required moot court program at Harvard Law School. It metamorphosed into book form twenty-seven years ago and has been revised five times since then, but not without significant help. We would like to thank Jeffrey Kobrick, Peter Murray, Charles Nesson, and Virginia Wise for advising us on the substantive chapters. Their knowledge and insights proved invaluable. Thanks also go to Gary Murphy, *The Bluebook* Editor of the *Harvard Law Review*, for his suggestions on updating the citation and style appendix. Finally, we are indebted to David Becker, Ames Fellow at Harvard Law School, and Scott McMillin, President of the Board of Student Advisers, for their comments and suggestions on final drafts of this edition.

Board of Student Advisers —
ITA Revision Committee
Heather Leal, Chair
Syrena Case
Barbara Fiacco
Joe Gershman
Marc Goldstein
Dana Kirchman
Kim Stallings

June 1996

SUMMARY OF CONTENTS

TABLE OF CONTENTS

TABLE OF CONTENTS

TABLE OF CONTENTS

TABLE OF CONTENTS

TABLE OF CONTENTS

INTRODUCTION

TO

ADVOCACY

RESEARCH, WRITING, AND ARGUMENT

CHAPTER 1

Interpreting Facts and Developing Core Theory

Legal problems come in all shapes and sizes. They may be complex or simple; interesting or mundane; novel or familiar. Money, lives, property, and values are all stakes at different times. The way you approach a legal problem depends on the contours of that problem and on your advocacy style. This chapter presents different ways of approaching legal problems. Although it focuses on a fictional appellate case used in a law school moot court program, *Bell-Wesley v. O'Toole*, the techniques apply across a range of situations.

In *Bell-Wesley v. O'Toole*, Rebecca and Scott Bell-Wesley sued Dr. Stephen O'Toole for damages arising from his negligent performance of a vasectomy and sperm count. These injuries included damages suffered by the Bell-Wesleys during Rebecca Bell-Wesley's subsequent pregnancy and childbirth, as well as future damages associated with the cost of raising their healthy son to majority. Although the trial court found that Dr. O'Toole had been negligent, the court limited the Bell-Wesleys' recovery to out-of-pocket costs, pain and suffering, emotional trauma, lost earnings, and loss of consortium for a total damage award of $100,000. The Bell-Wesleys appealed the decision on the grounds that the trial court improperly failed to recognize child-rearing costs as an element of damages in a wrongful pregnancy action. The Court of Appeals for the State of Ames affirmed the trial court's decisions of law. You are brought into the problem after the Ames Supreme Court has granted certiorari. Damages in a wrongful pregnancy action are an issue of first impression in the State of Ames. Thus, whether you represent Dr. O'Toole or the Bell-Wesleys, you must solve the legal problem using the facts, policy, case law, and creativity. You should use *Bell-Wesley v. O'Toole* to understand the many principles we will suggest in this book.

Most legal projects begin with the facts. In moot court competition, as in real-life appeals, the record is the lawyer's sole source of information about the facts of a case. The record for the appeal compiles all of the legal and factual determinations made by the lower court and includes the various pleadings and motions that the parties filed in the lower court, as well as the trial transcript, affidavits of various witnesses, and the lower court's opinion. In a moot court record, the various documents usually appear in abbreviated form. An actual record can be thousands of pages; the usual moot court record will be much shorter. The sample record in *Bell-Wesley v. O'Toole*, which can be found in Appendix B, is a typical example.

1

In other legal writing projects, such as briefs written for a trial court, the facts may come from a combination of sources, including interviews with the client or witnesses and discussions with colleagues. A clear understanding of the facts is essential as you begin your journey into both legal research and the process of developing a theory of the case, or your "core theory." (*See* this chapter, Part II, "Developing a Core Theory," p.3.)

Remember throughout the process of reading the facts, exploring your core theory, and beginning your legal research, that there are many solutions and approaches to every legal problem and set of facts. Creativity is often the key to developing an interesting and credible approach to your case.

I.   Facts in Context

The facts are one of the lawyer's most powerful weapons when coupled with supportive case law and a core theory. Like using any weapon, training is essential, especially in understanding the dual nature of facts.

Contrary to your initial impression, facts are neither static nor subject to only one interpretation. It is your job to examine critically the facts presented in order to discover which ones are important to your case. The context or background story will often shape which facts are important and the interpretation you give those facts.

For example, consider the fairy tale of *Goldilocks and the Three Bears*. From the bears' perspectives, the important facts are that they came home to find their house a wreck, their food eaten, and a potentially dangerous intruder passed out in their bedroom — an open and shut case for breaking and entering, robbery, and trespass. From Goldilocks' perspective, she was starving and near death, barely making it to the door of the bears' home. To avoid death, she entered the house, drank some soup, and passed out from the cold in a bed. She had no malicious intentions and simply did what was necessary to survive. The import of the same facts changed when examined against the background story. For the bears, the story was one of a grievous violation to the sanctity of their home. For Goldilocks, the story was one of necessity.

As you review your case, endeavor to see the facts from differing perspectives. In order to make compelling arguments, you need to develop an appropriate and credible narrative which forms the basis of your core theory, as well as the fact section of your brief. (*See* Chapter 4, "Writing a Brief," Part II, Section C, p.44.) In *Bell-Wesley v. O'Toole*, an undisputed fact is that Rebecca Bell-Wesley gave birth to a healthy baby boy, Frank Michael Bell. Dr. O'Toole views the birth as a benefit to the Bell-Wesleys who had tried unsuccessfully to conceive a healthy child over a period of years. For the Bell-Wesleys, however, the conception and birth of their

son violated a conscious choice they had made to forego having children; interrupted their lives; and changed them irrevocably. These alternate views of Frank's birth will influence the way each side addresses the legal problem.

Finally, remember that the legal research and writing process is dynamic. Your understanding of the facts will often change, sometimes radically, from the first time you read the facts, through your legal research, and finally as you draft the written material. A clear understanding of the facts is always essential, but the context and importance of many of the facts will be influenced by your core theory, the existing case law, and perhaps, scholarly work in the area. Be prepared to revise and re-evaluate your interpretation of the facts in order to make the strongest arguments for your client.

II.   Developing a Core Theory

In considering the facts and law pertinent to your case or project, you should begin to develop an overarching theory of the case, called the "core theory." The core theory is the foundation of your position. It is the unifying theme of your argument around which you present all issues and formulate all arguments.

Work on the core theory begins when you read the facts and continues throughout the process of legal research and writing. As you begin to think about the case, consider first the non-legal reasons that justify a decision in your favor. For example, consider the policy implications, the fairness considerations, and the proper role of the courts in deciding this and similar issues arising in the future. Many of these considerations will be addressed by other cases discussing your issue. They are often fact-based and logical. The core theory is the single idea which leaves the greatest impression on those who read or listen to your arguments.

Developing the core theory takes time and thought. Throughout your work, think about the arguments you generate from the record and your research. Try to structure your ideas around a theory that captures the essence of your case. The more difficult task is articulating your core theory into a narrative of several words or sentences. The process of distilling your ideas into a few sentences will produce the strand that connects your ideas into a cohesive whole and is often one of the more challenging and important parts of legal problem solving. (Sample core theories for the parties in *Bell-Wesley v. O'Toole* can be found in this chapter, Part III, Section H, "Develop a Core Theory," p.9.)

Core theory is a difficult concept for many law students to grasp, because they want to make arguments based solely on the legal standards they find during their legal research. However, your experience in other first-year classes should show the importance of core theory. First-year law students quickly discover that very similar facts applied to the same legal standard lead to radically different outcomes. It is often the core theory — the policy considerations, fairness considerations, and sometimes simple common sense — which drives judges. The development of a core theory that is compelling, logical, and appealing is one of the most important parts of legal thinking and analysis, because moot court and other legal projects will almost always prompt questions on which the law is unsettled.

III.   The Process of Reading the Record

There is no single way to read and understand the facts in the form of a record. While the following approach is geared toward preparing for an appellate case, the ideas presented apply generally to any legal research project.

     A.   Read the entire record.

     B.   Read the rules.

     C.   Sketch a chronology or diagram of what happened.

     D.   Narrow the issues for appeal and begin considering core theory.

     E.   Consider the standard of appellate review.

     F.   Formulate arguments.

     G.   Connect the facts to the legal issues.

     H.   Develop a core theory.

     I.   Consider opposing arguments and core theories.

     J.   Review the record with an eye toward your core theory and the facts most damaging to your side.

A. READ THE ENTIRE RECORD

Before trying to distill and narrow the information available to you in the record, you must have a broad overview of the case. A first read-through, even a fairly quick one, will help you to understand what is happening both legally and factually. With a broad overview, you can begin to narrow the legal and factual problems for the appeal.

Your job on appeal is to examine the lower court's decision closely to determine the precise legal grounds for the opinion, the potential issues of reversible error, and the available arguments for your position. Because the record is your only source of factual information, a mastery of the record is a prerequisite to an effective appeal.

B. READ THE RULES

This is often a good time to familiarize yourself with the rules of your particular court, be it moot or otherwise. Doing so now will help avoid unnecessary shocks down the line. The rules will supply information about deadlines, page limits, format, and the sources you may consult. Follow them carefully. While these guidelines are usually included with moot court documents, you should be aware that "real" rules are contained both in national compilations, such as the Federal Rules of Appellate Procedure, and local or circuit rules.

C. SKETCH A CHRONOLOGY OR DIAGRAM OF WHAT HAPPENED

The items in a record are not necessarily arranged in the order in which events actually happened. By preparing a chronology of events, you will have a comprehensive and detailed understanding of the factual setting. This is important because many cases turn not on what happened, but when it happened.

For example, in *Bell-Wesley v. O'Toole,* one of the important issues in determining whether damages should be awarded is whether Frank's birth harmed Rebecca Bell-Wesley's career goals. You need to examine the trial record of Rebecca's testimony to learn about her potential lost career opportunities. A reading of the record shows that Rebecca became pregnant after she accepted a new position at the attorney general's office. This is very important, because if Rebecca had become pregnant before she accepted the new position, she would be less likely to claim damages successfully.

In determining the factual history of the case, you will also discover what facts you do not have. In any court record, moot or otherwise, some facts will be missing or ambiguous. Once you notice what facts are missing, look more closely at the record to see if these facts are hidden or if they can be reasonably inferred from available facts. Facts inferred from the record should become a part of your argument and may be introduced in the Statement of Facts. If you choose to include them in the Statement of Facts, be sure to preface them in a way that signals to the court that you are making an inference. The misuse of facts or the use of inference as undisputed fact will hurt your credibility with the court.

As you read the record, be aware of the varying importance the court attaches to each fact. Typically, the appellate court will give the greatest weight to the findings of fact of the lower court. The extent to which the appellate court defers to the lower court's findings of fact is dependent

upon the standard of review that the appellate court adopts for the issue. (*See* this part, Section E, "Consider the Standard of Appellate Review"; Chapter 4, "Writing a Brief," Part II, Section D(3), p.49.) In reviewing the findings of fact in a civil case, the appellate court will review the facts of the case as presented in the plaintiff's complaint, in the defendant's answer, and in trial transcripts. The facts presented by the parties and witnesses are less significant than the findings of fact of the trial judge and jury. However, facts that are stipulated by both parties are undisputed and, therefore, are not reviewed by the appellate court.

D. NARROW THE ISSUES FOR APPEAL AND BEGIN CONSIDERING CORE THEORY

The lower court decides many issues. In narrowing the issues for appeal, focus on policy, legal, and factual questions raised by the record. On appeal, the legal issues are normally narrower and more defined than at the lower court level.

Determine which of the lower court's decisions are at issue on appeal so that you can concentrate on relevant facts and legal questions. Sometimes the court will limit the issues for you, as on the last page of the *Bell-Wesley v. O'Toole* record. (*See* Appendix B, p.121.) After reading these narrowed issues, you know that you need not consider the possible negligence arguments concerning the vasectomy.

The best places to discover the relevant legal and factual issues on appeal are in the lower court opinion and in the certified questions. They discuss the reasons for the court's ruling and should frame the issues for appeal. In *Bell-Wesley v. O'Toole*, the judge's fifth and sixth conclusions of law point you to the two vital issues on appeal: Can there be damages for a "wrongful pregnancy," and what items should enter into the calculation of these damages? (For the conclusions of law of the trial court in *Bell-Wesley v. O'Toole*, see the Record in Appendix B, p.113.)

In other cases, the opinion and record will not frame the issues so clearly, but a careful reading of the relevant documents should provide you with the important legal issues for the appeal. In non-moot court contexts, the narrowing of the issues may be considerably more difficult and may require legal research. Additionally, consider that many times non-moot court assignments will not be on appeal but rather posed in a posture more like law firm work. For example, if you are given a set of facts and asked to determine if there is a legal claim, the issues and legal theories may be quite undefined until a significant amount of research has been done.

In narrowing the issues, you will also be presented with policy implications which should prompt further consideration of your core theory. *Bell-Wesley v. O'Toole* presents several policy issues:

- Should society allow parents, who wish to keep their child, to force the doctor who negligently performed a vasectomy to pay for all of the costs parents normally incur in raising a child?

- What impact would such payment have on a child?

- What impact would such payment have on the medical profession?

- Would a decision against the doctor make it more difficult to find another doctor willing to perform a sterilization procedure?

- Were the parents actually traumatized by the birth, despite the fact that they had attempted to have children before opting for sterilization?

You need not, and probably cannot, determine all of the issues presented by the case before beginning research. Indeed, in the course of your research you should continuously refine issues and consider new ways of looking at the case. Legal research is a dynamic process of defining issues, developing arguments, and finding support for those arguments. You will inevitably reformulate issues and arguments as you discover the content of statutes and case law.

E.   CONSIDER THE STANDARD OF APPELLATE REVIEW

Another issue you should consider as you read the record is the applicable standard of review. The standard of review defines the extent of the actions an appellate court can take with respect to the issues before it, as well as the deference it must give the lower courts' decisions. An appellate court invariably wants to know what elements of the trial court decision you want it to review. One common question asked by moot court judges is "Counsel, what is it you want us to do here?" In some instances, the standard of review will be mentioned in the record, generally as part of the questions certified for appeal. When the standard of review is not stipulated, you should research it as you would any other legal issue.

Potential standards of review run the gamut from "de novo" review to "abuse of discretion" or "clearly erroneous" review. Appellate courts nearly always examine legal issues de novo; thus, you should cull the legal findings from the factual findings of the lower court. The standard of review will have implications for both your written and oral advocacy. For example, if you are arguing that there was an abuse of discretion at the trial court level you may wish to argue that the appellate court should decide the factual issues de novo. Thus, you will want to focus your arguments on the facts, perhaps at the expense of policy or legal arguments.

Standard of review is irrelevant where a higher court is not actually reviewing a lower court's ruling. For example, if a lower court certifies a question to a higher court, standard of review is inapplicable. Thus, you will only use standard of review in the appellate context.

F.   FORMULATE ARGUMENTS

The arguments you make in your written and oral presentation to the court answer the questions raised by the issues in your case and presented in the "Questions Presented" section of the brief. (*See* Chapter 4, "Writing a Brief," Part II, Section A, p.41.) These arguments provide the reasons the court should find in your favor.

Formulating arguments is a process, involving reason and analysis, as well as reliance on authority. The preparation of arguments should be in conjunction with the development of the core theory, which links all parts of your legal argument. You should try to consider some of the strong arguments before heading to the library. Don't be afraid to rely on your intuition. Begin thinking of how you can best frame the arguments for (and against) the position you wish to support. This list of potential sources for arguments will help generate some ideas:

- Arguments based on common sense notions of justice and equity — often one's client got into a predicament through a good-faith belief about the correctness of a certain action;

- Arguments based on authorities and case law that you have already studied;

- Arguments by analogy or comparison to other cases and situations with which you are familiar;

- Arguments typically associated with the subject matter of the case;

- Arguments based on the potential consequences of the court finding or not finding your way;

- Arguments affecting public policy.

This list is a starting point for research. During the course of your research, you will discover new argument categories to add to the list and reject some as frivolous. As you can see, many of the argument considerations are also those which drive the core theory.

G.   CONNECT THE FACTS TO THE LEGAL ISSUES

By now, you have a solid grasp of what actually happened and a basic understanding of the legal considerations. At this point, you should synthesize the two sets of information. As will be discussed in Chapter 3,

"Writing a Legal Research Memorandum"; Chapter 4, "Writing a Brief"; and Chapter 5, "Oral Argument," the key to an effective argument will be your ability to relate the legal arguments to the specific factual situation.

This requires you to look critically at the information in the record to determine which facts matter the most to your arguments. In this case, not every fact concerning Dr. O'Toole's performance of the vasectomy is relevant. Important facts are those that demonstrate how the wrongful pregnancy of a child can be a real injury to the parents. Examples of the economic and emotional cost to Rebecca and Scott Bell-Wesley can be used for this purpose.

The process of relating the facts to the law helps you continually redefine the factual and legal issues. There is a symbiosis between the facts and the legal issues. The important facts are important are determined by the legal issues, and the legal issues are determined by the facts of the case. Neither can be evaluated in a vacuum and both must be constantly considered and reconsidered in light of the core theory.

H. DEVELOP A CORE THEORY

After identifying the legal, factual, and policy issues, and generating a series of useful arguments, try to unite them into your core theory.

Any case can give rise to a number of alternative core theories. Here are some examples of what a core theory could look like for the appellant and appellee in *Bell-Wesley v. O'Toole*:

Appellant:

```
The Bell-Wesleys' wrongful pregnancy claim is
indistinguishable from any other medical malpractice
claim. They must be compensated for all of the
injuries flowing from Dr. O'Toole's repeated negli-
gence and the resulting birth of a child after they
had chosen to lead a childless lifestyle.
```

Appellee:

```
The Bell-Wesleys should not be awarded damages to
pay for the costs of raising their son, because they
wanted a healthy child.  Rather than being injured
by his birth, the Bell-Wesleys benefited from the
birth; it would be socially unacceptable for Dr.
O'Toole to compensate the parents for the birth of
their healthy son.
```

I.   CONSIDER OPPOSING ARGUMENTS AND CORE THEORIES

Anticipating the opposing side's arguments allows you a window into the thinking of your opponent and an opportunity to reassess your arguments and core theory. Although the facts and legal issues are the same for both parties, the manner in which they are interpreted, developed, and presented will differ.

The opposing party will present the facts and draw inferences in a light most favorable to its arguments. Likewise, they will select those arguments that most strongly support their core theory. Consider what that core theory might be and identify the possible arguments that make it work. By anticipating the opposing arguments and core theory, you can identify weaknesses in your own arguments and core theory.

It is not essential that you present arguments in your brief responding to each potential argument of the opposing party. Some believe that briefs should be "like two ships passing in the night," never addressing each other's arguments. Others believe you should make a strong case for your opponent and then tear it down. There are many uses for your opponent's arguments; how you utilize them is part strategy and part personal choice. Initially, however, you should strive to make the strongest arguments you can for your side, while taking into consideration the possible arguments for the other side. Then contemplate whether you want to make more structural changes in response to your opponent's arguments. Even if all of the arguments are not included in your brief, they might be raised during oral argument.

J. REVIEW THE RECORD WITH AN EYE TOWARD YOUR CORE THEORY AND THE FACTS MOST DAMAGING TO YOUR SIDE

Reading the record repeatedly will enhance your understanding of the facts. You may discover inconsistencies and omissions in the record as you become more familiar with it. The better you understand these problems, the better your ability to confront them. This is probably the most tedious step in the process, but it is important nonetheless.

A comprehensive understanding of the record, as well as the major arguments, will facilitate the initial stages of research. That understanding will enable you to focus your research and plot a logical course of action. By simply rushing to the library without carefully considering the intricacies and nuances that are bound to exist in the record, you may find yourself exploring many unproductive paths. This is not to suggest that you should not modify your research strategy as you delve into the cases and references, but that your research will be more efficient and effective from the outset if you begin with a solid understanding of the case.

This approach to beginning your legal research project is only one approach and is probably more regimented than the process one would normally follow. Consideration of the facts, core theory, policy, and legal arguments is ongoing. It is the dynamic nature of a legal problem which is often its most interesting and challenging aspect.

IV.   Sample Record: *Bell-Wesley v. O'Toole*

The sample moot court record for *Bell-Wesley v. O'Toole* appears in Appendix B. Examine it carefully to see what documents it includes and what factual and legal issues it raises. Note especially that instructions on the last page limit the issues available to moot court participants;   for example, whether the doctor's performance of the sterilization operation was negligent is not an issue. This type of constraint is common in moot court programs where skill development is more important than an exhaustive consideration of all possible issues.

Once you are familiar with the *Bell-Wesley v. O'Toole* record, you may want to compare your understanding of the facts and legal issues with the Questions Presented and the Statements of the Case in the sample briefs in Appendix E.

CHAPTER 2

Legal Research

I.   Introduction

Once you are familiar with the record and have given some consideration to a core theory, you are ready to begin the legal research phase of advocacy. The basic objective of legal research is to find primary authorities (cases, statutes, and regulations) to support a legal position. "Binding" or "mandatory" authorities are those that all lower courts and administrative bodies in a jurisdiction must follow. For example, the United States Supreme Court's decisions on federal law are binding on all federal and state courts. "Persuasive" authorities carry a great deal of weight because of the authoritativeness of the court or the organization that created them, but need not be followed in the jurisdiction in which you are working. Decisions on federal law by the United States Court of Appeals for the First Circuit are binding authority for all federal district courts in the First Circuit, but those decisions are merely persuasive authority for the other federal courts of appeals and district courts. In *Bell-Wesley v. O'Toole*, there is no binding authority for several reasons: (1) the mythical State of Ames does not generate case law or statutes; (2) the issue is one of "first impression," meaning that even if Ames did have authority, it would not be applicable; and (3) federal court cases cannot dictate the result in a state tort case.

This short guide to legal research introduces the elements of legal research and describes the standard legal sources. While the final goal of any legal research is to find law in the form of cases, statutes, and regulations, secondary sources may be very helpful in finding and understanding that law. Because law is a heavily published field, the efficient researcher surveys secondary sources for information that has already been compiled by someone else. Not only will these sources reduce the time needed to sift through indexes and to conduct ill-targeted computer searches, but the overview provided may also help you digest the substance of primary sources more easily. Legal publications are part of a large, interconnected system. There are many paths into this system, and once you have found one fruitful path or source, all others are readily accessible. The key is to understand the relationships among these sources. The following is a simplified research strategy model to use as a starting point. It will provide an overview of the sources available and suggest tips to make your legal research effective and efficient.

II.   Where to Begin

If the topic is an unfamiliar one, getting a general sense of the substantive area of the research question before launching into a detailed search will save time. Secondary sources such as law review articles and *American Law Reports* annotations will outline important issues and include specific legal terms that may help focus your search for the most relevant materials. A secondary source's treatment of the issue may help hone a core theory from a general "fairness" or "justice" argument into the most viable legal arguments. A good secondary source may also highlight whether the main issues are controversies in state or federal law and in cases or statutes. The *Bell-Wesley* case deals with the issue of wrongful pregnancy. Wrongful pregnancy is an example of a tort question left to the states, some of which have statutes governing the availability of the cause of action. Below is a brief introduction to secondary sources, loosely arranged in order of usefulness for an efficient legal research assignment.

A. LAW REVIEW ARTICLES

Law review articles offer succinct, yet full perspectives on cutting edge legal issues. Law reviews are periodicals produced at law schools and generally edited by students. They contain articles, notes, case comments, and book reviews typically written by professors, judges, and students. A law review article can be a general discussion of law in a specific subject area, a survey of law in one jurisdiction, or a more specific analysis of one important case. Usually written from a single perspective, an article advances and supports arguments about what the state of the law in an area should be. Because law reviews are published several times a year, they are the best source of current debate on legal issues. Generally, these journals are available in law libraries. In addition, the full text of articles in many law reviews is available on WESTLAW and LEXIS; the online availability of student-written notes, comments, and book reviews is more limited.

Law review articles can be retrieved through two different paper indexes: the *Index to Legal Periodicals and Books (ILP)* and the *Current Law Index (CLI)*. Both publications list articles according to subject matter, title, and author in the same manner that the *Reader's Guide to Periodical Literature* or *Magazine Index* gives access to magazine articles. Paper supplements to these guides are issued monthly, cumulated quarterly, and then issued annually as bound volumes. For the most recent publications available, check each non-cumulative supplement published after the last bound volume. *CLI* is more comprehensive than *ILP*, indexing over 900 legal periodicals. However, it only covers articles published after 1980. *CLI*'s online companion index, the Legal Resource Index (LRI), is available on some library computer systems and on WESTLAW (database identifier LRI). On LEXIS, the comparable index database is available in

13

the LAWREV library in the LGLIND file. Both online services also have databases to search the full text of journal articles on a particular topic, rather than the abstracts found in the Legal Resource Index. Unless you are looking for a very specific application of the law, a search of LRI's abstracts is generally more effective and comprehensive than a search of a full text database.

B. *AMERICAN LAW REPORTS*

Lawyers Cooperative publishes *American Law Reports* (*A.L.R.*) which includes a series of brief discussions about specific points of law arising in recent court cases. Generally, an entry includes the text of a major case on a given legal issue followed by an "annotation," a synopsis of all American law on that narrow topic that contains notes on parallel cases in other jurisdictions. On the wrongful pregnancy issue in the *Bell-Wesley* case, the Fourth Series of *A.L.R.* (*A.L.R.4th*) uses *Burke v. Rivo*, a 1990 Massachusetts Supreme Judicial Court case, as the primary case on the issue of wrongful birth and follows with a thirty-two page annotation entitled "Recoverability of Cost of Raising Normal, Healthy Child Born as Result of Physician's Negligence or Breach of Contract or Warranty." This annotation is particularly helpful to the research process because it explains the evolution of a "wrongful pregnancy" action and notes that early cases on this issue may be categorized as "wrongful birth" actions. The annotation includes a table of contents, a topical index and a jurisdictional index in order to quickly refer to a specific jurisdiction's cases as discussed in the text. See Illustrations #1B – 1E in Appendix C for sample pages from this wrongful pregnancy annotation. In addition, the pocket part, a paper pamphlet found at the back of the bound volume to update that volume, includes an annotated list of wrongful birth cases decided since the publication of the bound volume. The *2d–5th* Series of *A.L.R.* as well as *A.L.R. Federal* are available on LEXIS in the ALR library, ALR file.

To find useful annotations, start with the multi-volume *A.L.R. Index*, a subject-matter compilation of all the *A.L.R.* annotations. It includes annotations from the second through the current fifth series, the *A.L.R. Federal Series*, as well as case annotations which appear following cases in the *Lawyers Edition* of the U.S. Supreme Court Reports. Check the pocket part in order to access the most recent annotations. As an alternative to the *A.L.R. Index*, use the one-volume *Quick Index*, which covers *ALR 3d–ALR 5th Series*. A page of the *Quick Index* is included as Illustration #1A in Appendix C. Under the topics "Pregnancy," "Birth Control," "Sterilization," "Vasectomies," and "Wrongful Birth," the *A.L.R.* citation for the above annotation is found (in this case, 89 *A.L.R.4th* 632); this citation includes the volume number of the specific series and the page number on which the entry begins. Before finding this entry, you should check the "Annotation History Table" in the back of the *A.L.R. Index* (and its pocket part) to ensure that this annotation has not been supplemented or superseded by later annotations.

Another tool to access *A.L.R.* annotations is the *A.L.R. Digest*. This digest system uses its own system of topics to compile summaries of cases discussed in *A.L.R.* When using *A.L.R.*, be aware that the digest system is based on traditional distinctions into which new areas of law do not easily fit. For example, wrongful birth cases are listed in the *A.L.R. Digest* topics of "Damages," "Negligence," and "Physicians and Surgeons." By contrast, the wrongful birth annotation is accessible in the *A.L.R. Index* under the more fact-specific categories such as "Sterilization" and "Vasectomies."

In addition to providing descriptions of relevant cases in many different jurisdictions, all *A.L.R.* annotations include cross-references to other Lawyers Cooperative publications, including *American Jurisprudence* (a legal encyclopedia discussed in this chapter, Part II, Section C), that may include additional information on the topic. Beginning with the 5th Series, *A.L.R.* also cross-references to the West Key Number system (discussed in this chapter, Part IV, Section B, p.19), allowing the legal researcher to access relevant portions of West publications. *A.L.R.* also includes recommended search terms for use with online databases.

C. LEGAL ENCYCLOPEDIAS

Legal encyclopedias provide general discussions of virtually all legal subjects. The two most common encyclopedias are *Corpus Juris Secundum* (*C.J.S.*), published by West Publishing, and *American Jurisprudence 2d* (*Am. Jur. 2d*), published by Lawyers Cooperative Publishing. Each publisher cross-references its set with its other publications. The national encyclopedias summarize the law of all states; this very general discussion provides a broad framework, but may not provide enough of the nuances of a given state's law to be helpful to a researcher focusing on one state. There are also encyclopedias designed for individual states where the bar is large enough to sustain such a market. State legal encyclopedias' frequent references to cases and to statutory law make them quite useful. Some state legal encyclopedias are available in the 2CNDRY library on LEXIS.

Encyclopedias are written in a narrative style. Each clause or sentence usually is justified with specific references to case law from the jurisdiction(s) covered. This narrative explanation of the law provides an overall framework for analysis and is the encyclopedias' chief advantage over the disjointed treatment of the law in case law digests (discussed in this chapter, Part IV, Section B(2), p.19). Digests are a highly organized collection of individual paragraphs, each of which summarizes a point of law in a particular case.

D. ADDITIONAL SECONDARY SOURCES

The Restatements of Law and treatises may also be helpful to the legal researcher. The Restatements of Law on basic common law topics have achieved quasi-primary status in substantive areas including agency,

contracts, torts, property, trusts, judgments, and conflicts of laws. The Restatements are often cited in legal arguments and opinions. Although they do not carry as much weight as primary sources, many states declare the common law as summarized in the Restatements to be law in their jurisdictions unless contrary to declared public policy. Restatements are available on both WESTLAW (database identifier REST-[subject]) and LEXIS (RESTAT file in BEGIN library). The individual Restatements were based on general trends in the development of the common law and were authored by committees of prominent scholars associated with the American Law Institute. Be aware that some Restatements have more than one version; thus, the *Restatement Second of Contracts* more accurately reflects current law and is more authoritative than the original *Restatement of Contracts*.

Treatises are scholarly publications that analyze a substantive area of the law with reference to case law and statutes. Some treatises are one-volume texts, such as West's *Nutshell Series* or a larger "hornbook," such as *Prosser and Keeton on the Law of Torts*. The *Nutshell Series* and hornbooks are written by prominent professors and tend to be tailored to law students. Others are multi-volume sets, such as Wright and Miller's *Federal Practice and Procedure*. Most treatises are not available online.

III.   Statutes

A review of secondary sources for information on your research topic should have provided you with a sense of the contours of the law on that substantive area and, possibly, on that area within the relevant jurisdiction. In addition, those sources probably highlighted some of the key court cases and statutes that created legal standards and rules applicable to your research question. You have developed a core theory within this context and are now ready to find support for that theory in additional cases and statutes. While a single case or statute may provide the answer to your research question, your analysis will more likely rely on a dynamic interaction between case law, statutes, and subsequent cases interpreting those statutes. Depending on the substantive area, secondary sources may lead to either case law or statutes. There is no "correct" place to look for primary sources; however, because a statute could invalidate a long line of case law in one sweep, and there is no legal source that indicates when a statute overrules prior case law, check statutory materials before investing a great deal of time digging for cases.

A. FEDERAL STATUTES

Statutes are published in several forms. When bills become law, the text of the law appears first as a paper pamphlet known as a "slip law," published in paperback pamphlets or available online. Recently enacted laws are available through "advance legislative services." The federal version is West's *United States Code Congressional and Administrative News*

(*USCCAN*) laws, numbered with "public law numbers" and published chronologically in monthly paperback pamphlets that are later compiled in bound volumes. The laws enacted during a legislative session are compiled chronologically in one *USCCAN* set. An important congressional committee report, often included with the text of the law, offers some legislative history of the law. On WESTLAW, recently enacted federal statutes are available in US-PL; the corresponding LEXIS file is PUBLAW in the GENFED library. The federal session laws are published chronologically as *U.S. Statutes at Large*. To access a session law on a particular topic, use the subject index at the end of the session law set.

The federal laws are published by subject as the *United States Code*. Each subject is designated as a "title"; for example, title 42 refers to all laws related to "Public Health and Welfare." Conversion tables at the end of the set allow the researcher to access the official citation of the statute from its public law number. The official set is updated with annual bound volume supplements. An annotated code includes court cases interpreting the statutory law (like those found in the digests) and is updated by pocket parts and pamphlet supplements much more often than the official code. At the federal level, West publishes the *United States Code Annotated*, available on WESTLAW as USCA. Lawyers Cooperative publishes the *United States Code Service*, available on LEXIS as the USCODE file in the GENFED library. Both sets include a general subject index to help you locate statutes applicable to your topic; in addition, each includes a popular name table that provides the official citations for statutes referred to by name, such as the Gramm-Rudman Act, rather than official name or number.

B. STATE STATUTORY MATERIALS

Research on recently enacted state laws is not so easily generalized as federal statutory research. The advance legislative services vary from state to state. On WESTLAW, the current state legislative service is available in [ST]-LEGIS; on LEXIS, the relevant file is [ST]-ALS in the LEGIS library. On WESTLAW, use the postal abbreviation of the relevant state in place of [ST]; LEXIS uses longer state abbreviations. All states publish their session laws, accessible through the subject index at the end of the set. While some states publish their official codes, other states rely solely on annotated codes published by private companies. The state code is available in [ST]-ST and the annotated code is available in [ST]-ST-ANN on WESTLAW. When you know the citation of the statute you want to read, use the "find" command with that citation to call up that document directly. For example, "find MN ST s145.424" in WESTLAW will retrieve Minnesota's Section 145.424 on wrongful birth. On LEXIS, there is mixed availability of state annotated and unannotated codes in the STATES library. These codes may be accessed through individual state libraries as well. To find the wrongful birth statute on LEXIS, use the command "LEXSTAT" with the proper citation of the statute, such as "LEXSTAT MN CODE 145.424."

Online services have tables of contents or indexes to the codes which may help you search by topic; WESTLAW indexes statutes in [ST]-IDX and allows a user to "jump" directly to the appropriate citation. As an alternative, search the text of a state code directly for relevant terms with a search under "wrongful birth" or "wrongful pregnancy." Use a field or segment search to search the text or heading of statutes while avoiding "false hits" from language found only in the annotations' case summaries.

When you begin a search for statutes applicable to your legal question, the annotated code provides the best starting point. In addition to the text of the statute, the annotated code is an excellent case-finding tool because it includes the most significant cases interpreting that statute. For example, Illustrations #2A and #2B in Appendix C include a page from the statutory set's index and the wrongful birth statute from the *Minnesota Annotated Statutes*. In the historical notes section, the annotated code lists the session law numbers of prior amendments of the statute. Through these citations, you can trace the development of the statute to its current form. Related statutes and administrative regulations, relevant law review articles, and citations to *A.L.R.* and legal encyclopedias are listed in the "cross references" section. To update your search in the annotated code, check the pocket parts and paperback supplements which include laws enacted since the last edition of the annotated code. At the beginning of the pocket part or paper supplement, the "closing tables" indicate the most recent session laws covered by that publication. For more recently enacted laws, check the paper version of the advance legislative service, which is also available on WESTLAW and LEXIS.

IV.   Cases and Case-Finding Tools

A. WHERE THE CASES ARE LOCATED

Federal and state courts create case law by issuing opinions. Although the federal and state governments often publish cases, most legal materials come from commercial publishers. Individual decisions are often first issued in official form as pamphlets or "slip opinions." They are then cumulated chronologically in bound volumes. Interim pamphlets, known as "advance sheets," are published between the individual slip decisions and the final bound volumes. The advance sheets provide the official reporter citation for the case because they use the same page numbering of the forthcoming official volume. Chronological volumes of decisions are known as "reports" or "reporters." Formerly, every state issued "official," *i.e.* governmentally published, reports of their highest court and sometimes of the intermediate appellate courts. Today, fewer than half of the states continue that practice, so the commercially published volumes are often the official state reporter. Typically, commercial publishers' regional or state reporters are available on the library shelf

more quickly than the official state reporters. While the text of the cases is identical in official and unofficial reporters, *The Bluebook,* a guide to uniform legal citation, states that all citations to cases decided by courts of the state in which the brief is filed should include citations to the official state reporter as well as the regional reporter. (*See* Appendix A, "General Rules of Style and Citation of Authorities," Part IV, Section A(1)(b), p.94.)

Federal court cases are published in federal reporters. District court opinions appear in the *Federal Supplement* (F. Supp.), published by West Publishing. Opinions written by the federal courts of appeals are published in the Federal Reporter. The *Federal Reporter* is currently in its third numbered series, abbreviated in citation form as "F.3d." The official decisions of the Supreme Court of the United States are known as *United States Reports* (U.S.). The West Publishing Company's version is the *Supreme Court Reporter* (S. Ct.) and the Lawyers Cooperative Publishing Company's set is called the *Lawyers Edition* (L. Ed.). *United States Law Week* is probably the most widely used weekly publication reporting the most important decisions at state and federal levels. It is predominantly used for its U.S. Supreme Court section, which contains cases before they appear in the advance sheets of the *Supreme Court Reporter* or *Lawyers Edition.*

The text of recent court decisions appears first on the online legal databases, WESTLAW and LEXIS, and can be retrieved through a subject search. (See the discussion of computer research in this part, Section C, "Computerized Research Strategies," p.22.) These services include opinions within several hours or days of a decision's issuance, depending on the court. Any of the parallel citations of the case may be used to call up the text of the court's opinion. On WESTLAW, the command "find" combined with the case citation calls up the text; on LEXIS, the comparable command is "LEXSEE." For example, if you found the citation to the "wrongful birth" case *Cockrum v. Baumgartner* in a digest, you could retrieve it on WESTLAW with the commands "fi 447 NE2d 385" or "fi 95 Ill2d 193"; on LEXIS, use "LEXSEE 447 NE2d 385" or "LEXSEE 95 Ill2d 193."

B. CASE-FINDING TOOLS

1. *Secondary Sources*

Law review articles, *A.L.R.*, legal encyclopedias, and other secondary sources all reference potentially useful cases. (For a full treatment of these sources, see this chapter, Part II, "Where to Begin," p.13.)

2. *Digests*

Digests provide subject access to case law through alphabetically arranged topics and numbered subtopics. Case holdings are summarized in short paragraphs under these topics and subtopics. A particular digest

covers all reported cases within its jurisdiction, including federal cases which originate in that state. This finding aid leads you to primary and secondary sources but does not provide either the text of the law or any analysis of it. There are digests for individual states, some regions (as defined by the regional reporter system), the federal courts, the U.S. Supreme Court, and state and federal courts combined. There are also separate digests for the topical reporters. Here are four simple steps to follow in using the digest system:

a. Make a Subject and Jurisdiction Determination

Determine the legal subjects you want to research and the jurisdictions in which you want to focus that research. For example, in *Bell-Wesley v. O'Toole*, you would be most interested in state law, because a tort action such as wrongful birth is created by state law. Federal cases that originate in a jurisdiction appear in that jurisdictional digest; for example, the Arizona state digest includes cases filed in federal district court in Arizona.

Because Ames is a mythical jurisdiction, counsel in *Bell-Wesley v. O'Toole* would be interested in the law of many states. If, however, the case were in an Illinois court, counsel could go directly to the *Illinois Digest* or the *Northeastern Reporter Digest*, which includes Illinois. A regional reporter digest abstracts case law from only those states covered by that regional reporter. The *Decennial Digests* provide a full survey of all state and federal case law beginning in 1896. Through the *Eighth Decennial Digest*, the *Decennial Digests* were true ten-year cumulations of all federal and state cases. With the Ninth, the so-called *"Decennial"* was divided into two separate cumulations, Part One and Part Two, each covering a five-year period. To supplement the five-year cumulations, West issues a volume of the *General Digest* about every six weeks. Each *General Digest* volume is a self-contained unit covering all topics from A to Z. To save you from having to examine each *General Digest* volume, every tenth volume (10th, 20th, etc.) contains a cumulative index indicating which volumes, if any, in those ten volumes contain particular topics and key numbers.

b. Descriptive Word Index

Located at the end of each set of digests, the Descriptive Word Index is an alphabetical listing of topics. The index contains both legal concepts and fact words, *e.g.*, "negligence" and "sterilization." With *Bell-Wesley* in mind, you could search under legal concepts, such as "Wrongful Conception" or "Wrongful Pregnancy," as well as under fact words like "Vasectomy." Note that a digest's categorizations often lag behind the current language used to describe the law; even though "wrongful birth" no longer accurately describes the Bell-Wesleys' cause of action, you may still have to use the dated phrase for legal research purposes. For example, under "Wrongful Birth," you will find, in bold print, the entry "Phys 18.110." This entry is the topic name ("Phys" stands for "Physicians and Surgeons")

and key number (18.110) for your subject. Record this information. For a parallel path, see Illustration #3A in Appendix C for the entry under "Vasectomy" in the Descriptive Word Index of the *Ninth Decennial Digest, Part 2, 1981–1986*.

c. Digests

Topics in the digests are arranged in alphabetical order by topic name, such as "Physicians and Surgeons." The following discussion is tailored to the West digest system; other digests are similarly organized with comparable number systems. Each topic is subarranged in numerical order by key number, such as the key number 18.110 for damages. For example, to find cases abstracted under "Physicians and Surgeons 18.110," first locate the digest volume containing the topic "Physicians and Surgeons." Once you have found that topic, search for the key number 18.110. It is in numerical order within the topic section. A collection of abstracts of cases relevant to your inquiry is listed under the key number. These abstracts are taken from the headnotes at the beginning of each case in the West reporter system. Each entry summarizes the particular point of law addressed in the case. After skimming the case abstracts in the main digest volume, always check the pocket part in the back of the volume for updated entries. In addition, check any pamphlet supplement.

A digest search turns up an abstract for a point of law that parents who have a healthy child cannot seek damages from a doctor who negligently performed a sterilization procedure. This case, *Cockrum v. Baumgartner*, appears to discuss wrongful birth actions directly, one of the issues identified at the very beginning of the *Bell-Wesley* research process. Illustration #3B in Appendix C includes the *Cockrum* abstract under "Physicians and Surgeons 18.110" in the *Ninth Decennial Digest, Part 2, 1981–1986*. Note that the case abstracts under each key number are arranged by the court that decided the case. Supreme Court cases are followed by federal courts of appeals cases, which are listed numerically by circuit. Thus, all Eleventh Circuit cases are listed together, beginning with the most recent decision. Next, federal district court decisions are arranged alphabetically by district. State court decisions are listed in alphabetical order by the name of the state, decisions by the highest state court appearing before those of the lower state courts. When more than one decision is listed for a court, those decisions appear in reverse chronological order.

d. Reporters

Use the citations to find the fully printed cases in the reporters. In this example, you would find *Cockrum v. Baumgartner* at 447 N.E.2d 385, in the *Northeastern Reporter, Second Series*, volume 447 at page 385, and at 95 Ill. 2d 193 in the *Illinois Reports, Second Series*, volume 95 at page 193. See Illustrations #4A and #4B in Appendix C for the first two pages of the

decision, including the headnotes and West topic and key numbers. Although the digests' case summaries provide important information for your research, you should not rely on them; read the entire decision. The case summaries are prepared by the commercial publishers. Although they are usually accurate, they cannot be considered statements of the law. Do not cite a case without reading all of it. Headnotes cannot capture critical nuances. The case summaries will not contain the kind of detail needed to determine how each case could be distinguished and differentiated; these are critical points to include in a legal memo or brief. (*See* Chapter 3, "Writing a Legal Research Memorandum," Part III, Section F, p.34; Chapter 4, "Writing a Brief," Part III, p.53.)

C. COMPUTERIZED RESEARCH STRATEGIES

Many lawyers today rely on the speed and accuracy of computerized databases in both the exploratory and final stages of their research. Because the computer can search rapidly through its vast memory in response to a search command, computer-aided research can quickly and effectively augment traditional research methods. The ease with which you may find opinions written by a particular judge or in a particular circuit on a specific topic make online resources extremely useful. Since databases are kept very current, computer searches are especially helpful for updating and for investigating newly emerging areas of the law. Be aware that the online databases include cases that are not published in the official reporters or that have been "depublished." These cases will not have a citation to F. Supp. or F.3d, but will only be cited by a WL (WESTLAW) or LEXIS number. Jurisdictions have different rules about the precedential value of unpublished or depublished decisions; therefore, research the court rules before citing an unpublished case.

One major drawback of online searches is the limited availability of older materials. Furthermore, unpredictable technical problems may prevent access to the online service. Finally, practitioners tend to limit their use of WESTLAW and LEXIS because of the expense of the services.

Online searching is ideal when you want to combine two or more concepts or facts, a process almost impossible to do using the linear approach of traditional hard copy indexes. Generally, online searches are most efficient when the facts are very specific or when the issues are quite narrow. When you are searching for a broad overview of a subject, hard copy secondary sources are preferable. In these instances, computer searches often dredge up too much material to be reviewed efficiently. Learning the individual features of each type of legal research tool in hard copy makes it much easier to deal with the online version effectively. With the ability to use hard copy and online databases, you will be able to make research decisions that are time efficient and cost effective.

To search efficiently online, first carefully choose the database in which you will conduct your search. Both online services offer specialized databases that compile cases in one field of law, such as family law for the *Bell-Wesley* project. WESTLAW is organized by database; LEXIS is divided into libraries, within which are more narrow files. Within these specialized databases, you may be able to specify whether you want family law cases from a given state, all state courts, all federal courts, or all state and federal courts. This service is particularly useful when you are researching a very narrow topic or a cutting-edge legal issue that has not yet been presented to most courts. A search with "wrongful pregnancy" and "vasectomy" will yield cases directly on point, whereas you may have to cull through many medical malpractice cases in the books before finding cases dealing specifically with negligent sterilization. Both online services offer menu screens immediately after you log into the service. Database identifiers are listed on these menus. To change databases within WESTLAW at any time, type "db" and the database identifier. Note that the "db" command by itself will return the researcher to the main menu. The corresponding LEXIS commands are ".cl" to change libraries and ".cf" to change files. These commands will return you to the main menu and the menu of the library, respectively. If you know the library or file you would like to access, type that identifier after the appropriate command.

Both WESTLAW and LEXIS offer two types of search methods in all of their databases. The first type, known as "Boolean" on LEXIS and "terms and connectors" on WESTLAW, is a special search language. It involves the use of commands like "and," "or," and more specialized commands like "/n" to search for two words or phrases within "n" words of each other. In addition, the commands "/s" and "/p" retrieve documents in which two words or phrases appear with the same sentence or the same paragraph, respectively. An added feature of WESTLAW is the ability to combine a West topic and key number with words likely to identify a specific fact pattern within that topic area; in this case, because the relevant key number highlights medical malpractice, a search incorporating it will avoid cases involving wrongful birth actions brought against pharmacists and manufacturers of surgical devices used in the sterilization process. The following searches would be fruitful for the *Bell-Wesley* research task:

```
LEXIS:      wrongful birth or wrongful conception or
            wrongful pregnancy and vasectomy or
            sterilization

WESTLAW:    "wrongful birth" or "wrongful
            conception" or "wrongful pregnancy"
            and vasectomy or sterilization

            299k18.110 and "wrongful birth" or
            "wrongful conception" or "wrongful
            pregnancy"
```

The second type of search is known as "FREESTYLE" on LEXIS and "natural language" on WESTLAW. This search method allows you to type in a sentence or question focused on your research task; the online service then identifies the words within that sentence that may find relevant cases. While a "terms and connectors" or Boolean search will find all cases with the relevant search terms, "natural language" and "FREESTYLE" have default maximum number of cases retrievable (usually twenty-five, but you can change this cap).

> LEXIS and WESTLAW: Can a doctor who negligently performs a vasectomy be held liable in a "wrongful pregnancy" action?

A "FREESTYLE" or "natural language" search is most useful in the early stages of research. The "Boolean" and "terms and connectors" searches, which offer the researcher the ability to construct focused searches, are more useful when you are familiar with the specific area in which you are conducting research and the relevant terms used within that substantive area. Because it can be both time-consuming and costly to read documents online, a narrow search is crucial to efficient legal research. Each online service has additional search tools designed to hone your searches. In order to develop solid research skills within each service, take advantage of the beginning and advanced training sessions offered by both WEST-LAW and LEXIS.

V.   Shepardizing

To determine whether cases on which you want to rely are still valid law — that they have not been reversed on appeal, overruled by a later court, or limited in subsequent decisions — you must consult *Shepard's Citations*. *Shepard's Citations* lists later opinions and law review articles that refer to the case or statute in which you are interested. *Shepard's* is also useful as a case-finding tool; once you have identified a source that is on point, a list of later cases that have cited your case may provide further insight, as well as more current articulations of the law. *Shepard's* has citators corresponding to each of the reporter systems in which a case may be cited (official reporters, unofficial reporters, specialty reporters, etc.). *Shepard's* also has citators chronicling treatment of the United States Constitution, federal statutes, federal regulations, and the Restatements of Law. Although there are *Shepard's* publications for statutes and regulations in addition to case citators, attorneys most often consult *Shepard's* to update case law.

Shepard's is published in hard cover volumes and updated with paper-back supplements. *Shepard's* volumes are not cumulative. Thus, each volume must be consulted to ascertain the precedential value of the case. The most recent supplement's cover includes a list of all volumes and

pamphlet supplements needed to do a complete search for your case. This list is entitled "What your library should contain." The color of the paperback supplement's cover indicates the extent of its coverage. While most *Shepard's* units are updated monthly with red paper or newsprint supplements, gold pamphlets usually indicate semi-annual supplements.

To Shepardize a case, such as *Cockrum v. Baumgartner*, 447 N.E.2d 385 (Ill. 1983), find the *Shepard's* set that covers Illinois cases. This Shepard's lists the case under its *Illinois Reports* citation as well as its *Northeastern Reporter* citation. In the *Northeastern Reporter, Second Series* section, look up volume 447, page 385 in the citator. In the heading of the case, Shepard's lists the title of the case, the date on which it was decided, and all parallel citations of the case and citations to the direct history of the case. Citations to subsequent court treatment of the case appear below this heading. *Shepard's* letter abbreviations appear to the left of the citations to indicate how the original case was treated. A list of the *Shepard's* abbreviations and their meanings is printed at the front of every *Shepard's* citator. For example, "r" means the case was reversed on appeal. Following the appellate history of the cited case, *Shepard's* lists other cases that cite the case but were not part of the original litigation. The conscientious researcher should check all cases with negative treatment codes, such as "overruled," "distinguished," "criticized," "limited," "questioned," or "explained." Because some courts will cite to only one reporter, especially when the official reporter lags behind the publication of the unofficial reporter, you should Shepardize both the official and unofficial versions of the state cases to identify all cases that refer to your case.

Once you have identified one relevant case, *Shepard's* is a good tool to find related cases. The shorter the citation list, the easier the task. To limit the task, identify the relevant headnotes from the original case. *Shepard's* lists corresponding superscript numbers after the reporter abbreviation in the *Shepard's* list. This superscript number indicates that the later court specifically cited the case for the particular issue raised in the headnote. Additionally, at the end of the list of citations, *Shepard's* includes a number of citations to law review articles and *A.L.R.* annotations that refer to the case. (*See* Appendix C, Illustration #5, p.134.)

Shepard's is simple and very efficient on both WESTLAW and LEXIS. To Shepardize a case online, type the command "sh" with the case citation. In order to retrieve only certain treatment codes in LEXIS, type ".se," then the treatment code, such as "r" for reversed, after you have retrieved the full Shepard's treatment of your case. In order to access only the negative history on WESTLAW, type "locate negative." In addition to *Shepard's*, WESTLAW offers InstaCite, a service that reports negative direct history, beginning in 1972. Direct history includes the subsequent treatment of the case on appeal or on remand. Be sure to look closely to determine whether the case has been overruled. Although InstaCite notes when a

case is overruled, it does so only with a small note. InstaCite also lists the case's parallel citation and citations to *C.J.S.* encyclopedia entries that cite the original case. LEXIS offers AutoCite, a service that compiles negative indirect history of cases. AutoCite lists parallel citations and *A.L.R.* citations, as well.

VI.   Overview of Research Tips

Consult secondary sources to determine key words to conduct your search, as well as to find citations to seminal cases or statutes. Keep track of each step of your research. As you focus your research, you will avoid duplicative searches by writing down the terms you used when accessing different indexes, tables of contents, and digests. At this point, if not before, you should be able to make a determination of whether to pursue state or federal law. Because a statute could overrule years of common law development in a specific substantive area, begin with a search of statutory law to determine whether a statute could govern your legal question. If a statute is on point, check the annotated code for cases that have interpreted and applied the statute. If no relevant statute is found, begin your search for relevant cases by using *A.L.R.* or a digest. Once you have found one relevant case, Shepardize that case to ensure that it is still good law and to find more recent cases on the same legal point. Follow up your search for case law with a WESTLAW or LEXIS search combining important words and/or West topics and key numbers. As you follow this generalized search pattern, be attentive to the cross-references within the relevant documents you find.

Because legal research often does not result in a simple and direct answer to your research question, knowing when to stop researching is one of the most difficult aspects of legal research. There are two general rules that offer some guidance. First, when the sources you have found cross-reference each other without significant reliance on unfamiliar sources, you probably have found the most important sources. To ensure that your research is up-to-date, you may want to use *Shepard's* online to find recent cases citing your major sources. The second rule is framed in economic terms: when the marginal value of an additional source is less than the work required to access that source, stop researching. Over time, you will develop a sense of when you have done enough research. However, one hard-and-fast rule is to keep notes of your research strategy so that you or a colleague can retrace your steps efficiently, if follow-up research is required.

VII.   Suggested Bibliography

Robert C. Berring, *Finding the Law* (10th ed. 1995). The most recent legal research text, this is a more condensed source than others discussed below. It offers abbreviated explanations of the legal sources, including cases, statutes, legislative history, and administrative materials, along with sample page illustrations.

Morris L. Cohen & Kent C. Olson, *Legal Research in a Nutshell* (5th ed. 1992). A concise guide to research designed as a quick introduction to a variety of legal sources.

Morris L. Cohen et al., *How to Find the Law* (9th ed. 1989). A very comprehensive source organized by types of document, such as cases, statutes, legislative history and administrative publication. A discussion of WESTLAW and LEXIS is integrated into the discussion of documents; however, it may be dated. The text also includes a chapter describing the context of legal sources, as well as a research strategy chapter. The appendices list state legal research guides, bibliographies and state primary legal sources.

Steven Emanuel, *LEXIS for Law Students* (2d ed. 1995). This step-by-step guide offers explanations of basic searching skills, explanations of how to find different types of legal documents on LEXIS, and research strategies in some specialized substantive areas. It also includes an introduction to other LEXIS products, including the NEXIS news service and Jurisoft products.

J. Myron Jacobstein et al., *Fundamentals of Legal Research* (6th ed. 1994). This is a current and comprehensive legal research text. It is organized by type of document and includes sample page illustrations for important legal sources. The book integrates its discussions of WESTLAW and LEXIS, but it also includes a separate chapter devoted to electronic research which allows comprehensive comparisons of the two databases' searching mechanisms.

Nancy P. Johnson et al., *Winning Research Skills* (2d ed. 1993). This concise text is tailored to first-year law students and introduces the basics of legal research with a focus on West publications. It includes a good discussion on how to integrate book and electronic research and an appendix focused on how to conduct a search in WESTLAW.

VIII.   Sample Research Pages

Sample pages from various legal sources appear in Appendix C. Look over the documents and note the relationships among the sources. For example, either *A.L.R.* or the *Decennial Digest* could lead the researcher to relevant cases in a number of jurisdictions. By Shepardizing one of the relevant cases and paying careful attention to the specific headnote cited in subsequent cases, you could find additional cases. Note once again that *Shepard's* does not include statutes that may displace the well-developed common law. For this reason, be sure to check your jurisdiction's statutory code. To maximize your research effort, check the annotated version of the code, which may lead to useful law review articles and cases interpreting the relevant statute.

CHAPTER 3

Writing a Legal Research Memorandum

I.   The Purpose of Memoranda

Memoranda (memos) are written for a variety of purposes. At the trial level, memos may be written before a lawsuit has begun, when a problem has arisen and an attorney must decide whether or not to take the case. In making this decision, a lawyer must consider possible claims arising from the fact pattern and how successful those claims are likely to be given statutory and case law in the jurisdiction. At the appellate level, where the causes of action are already defined, attorneys must present the existing law on those causes of action and identify and evaluate the legal arguments that may be made by both sides. Then, when it comes time to write a brief for the case, the attorney can decide which cases are most supportive of her side and present her strongest arguments, as well as distinguish the cases and counter the arguments presented by opposing counsel. This chapter focuses on memos at the appellate level. It suggests ways in which you might analyze and present the results of your legal research begun in Chapters 1 and 2.

II.   Comparing Memorandum Writing and Brief Writing

A legal memo of the type described in this chapter is an explanatory document. Unlike a brief, in which the writer attempts to persuade the reader to take a side by making strong arguments for one side and rebutting those of the other, a memo should present arguments objectively and then evaluate them. For example, in analyzing any given argument, a memo presents the strongest points for the appellant and the strongest points for the appellee. It indicates the strengths and weaknesses of each argument and the support or lack of support from case law: it argues both sides. While there are always two sides to an argument, one side may be stronger than the other. When one side has tremendous support from case law and the other side far less, you should make the imbalance clear to the reader. On the other hand, if precedent within the jurisdiction conflicts or there is no binding authority (*see* this chapter, Part III, Section F(3), "Use of Authority," p.37), this should be clear to the reader, as well. Furthermore, your memo should candidly assess the likelihood of your client prevailing. After reading a memo, the reader should have a good sense of the law that will apply to the fact pattern, as well as an idea of how a court is likely to apply the law in your jurisdiction.

A good legal memo concisely presents the relevant findings of your research and the legal and policy arguments that may be used by both sides. It provides the ideal foundation for writing a brief and for preparing for oral argument. The attorney for the Bell-Wesleys prepared for their appeal to the Ames Supreme Court by researching and writing the sample memo in Appendix D. Because the issue of child rearing damages in a wrongful pregnancy action is one of first impression in the State of Ames, the Bell-Wesleys' attorney surveyed case law in other states and then focused on detailing the reasons why the Ames Supreme Court might adopt one rule over another. Although you should view this sample as a guide to writing legal research memoranda, remember that your memos should be geared toward your specific project. Where your issue has been oft-litigated in your jurisdiction, you will have to spend much more time distinguishing unfavorable cases and analogizing favorable ones. Adjust your approach to meet the needs of the assignment.

Nonetheless, all good memos and briefs blend the facts of the case with the law. They show how the facts of previous cases and the case at hand compare, drawing analogies between some facts and distinguishing others. As in all legal writing, clarity and simplicity are required in both memos and briefs. Keep sentences short; do not assume your reader knows anything about your case or the causes of action involved; and explain concepts clearly. The primary difference between writing styles in the brief and the memo stems from their different purposes. Briefs are designed to persuade; memos, to explain law and policy. Thus, memos are written in a more objective style than are briefs.

III.   Parts of a Memorandum

Memo form differs dramatically depending on the purpose of the memo and the preferences of the person for whom it is written. The form described here is formal and comprehensive. Properly using the form presented here will require you to think carefully about the structure of the memo and the arguments within it. Such analysis is important regardless of the form you ultimately choose.

Memos often contain the following sections:
  A. Heading;
  B. Questions Presented;
  C. Brief Answers;
  D. Statement of Facts;
  E. Applicable Statutes (optional);
  F. Discussion (supported explanations of the Brief Answers);
  G. Conclusion; and
  H. Scope of Research.

An explanation of each section follows. The sections are addressed in the order in which they appear in the memo. However, you will probably not write the memo in that order. Outlining initial questions and writing a structured Discussion section are good first steps. With an idea of what you want to say and in what order you wish to say it, you can develop more specific questions for the Questions Presented section. The Brief Answers should generally be written last, as they are summaries of the Discussion section.

A. HEADING

Memos begin by identifying the person for whom they are written, the author, the date, and the subject. In inner-office memos, the subject may be a simple reference to a case name. It will often be more useful, however, to include topics covered by the memo in the "Subject" section. The memo you write may address issues important in other cases. If your memo can be filed by subject, other attorneys may access it more easily. The date is more important than you might think — precedent changes. Thus, your memo may well need updating before your case comes before a court.

B. QUESTIONS PRESENTED

The Questions Presented perform two primary functions for the reader of the memo: (1) they inform the reader of the specific legal questions that the memo will answer and that arise from the facts of the case; and (2) they define the organizational structure of the memo. The memo answers the questions in the order asked.

While the questions come first in a memo, you will need to do substantial research and probably some writing before you are ready to draft them. You will begin your research with basic questions: What constitutes a successful cause of action? What is the law in the relevant jurisdiction? What legal and policy arguments may be made to support either side? While useful as you perform research and begin to write your Discussion section, these are not the types of questions that belong in the Questions Presented section. Once you have finished outlining or writing the Discussion section, review it and formulate questions that clearly present the specific legal issues that your Discussion addresses. Usually, one to three questions will suffice. By requiring you to determine the precise legal issues to be answered in the memo and the order in which you will present the answers to those questions, the Questions Presented force you to develop a clear, structured memo. You may find, as you begin formulating your questions, that the memo will be more clear to the reader if structured somewhat differently. Thus, going back and forth between writing the Discussion section and developing the Questions Presented may be useful.

The author of the *Bell-Wesley* memo chose a single, broad question for the Question Presented. Because her task was to assess the likelihood of the Ames Supreme Court adopting a full recovery damages rule in wrongful pregnancy causes of action, she had to survey the possibilities across jurisdictions. Her single question reflects the broad scope of her research and answer.

```
Can the parents of a healthy, normal child, born
subsequent to a negligently performed sterilization
operation, recover the cost of raising the child in
a wrongful pregnancy action?
```

(*See* Appendix D, p.136.)

The author could have chosen to use two questions, the first asking if there was a cause of action, given the facts of the case; the second, what recovery would be possible. However, the cause of action in this case was well-established and only required a paragraph of explanation in the memo. The question provides an outline for the memo — after reading it, it is clear that the author will focus primarily on potential damages.

C. BRIEF ANSWERS

While this section precedes the Discussion section, it should be written after the Discussion section has been written. In this section, briefly summarize the answers that your memo provides to the Questions Presented. Include a very short and general explanation of the grounds on which the questions are answered. Do not include references to specific cases — your reader can get cites and more detailed information from your Discussion section. Everything included in your Brief Answers section should be elaborated upon in the Discussion.

Remember that your Brief Answers (and your Discussion) should actually answer the Questions Presented. The reader, understanding the legal issues raised after reading your Questions Presented, should be able to find the answers immediately in your Brief Answers.

Notice how the Brief Answer in the *Bell-Wesley* memo answers the Question Presented directly. Recall, the question was whether the parents, given the facts of the case, could recover the costs of raising the child.

```
Yes.   However, child-rearing damages are unlikely
in the Bell-Wesley case.  This issue is one of first
impression in Ames; other jurisdictions are divided.
A majority of jurisdictions do not allow any recovery
for child-rearing costs.   Five jurisdictions re-
quire that such a recovery be offset by the benefit
the parents will receive from the child in the form
```

```
of aid and affection (the "benefit rule").    Two
jurisdictions provide for full recovery of the costs
of raising a child to majority.
```

(*See* Appendix D, p.136.)

After reading the Question Presented and the Brief Answer, the reader knows exactly what the memo covers and what conclusions are drawn. In addition, the memo structure is clear: the majority of jurisdictions denying benefits will be discussed first; then, the five governed by the benefit rule; and finally, the two that provide full recovery.

D. STATEMENT OF FACTS

Briefly summarize the facts that are relevant to all potential causes of action and that are required to explain the story to the reader. Be objective in your presentation: you are not trying to sway your reader or to make arguments here, you are merely trying to convey the facts relevant to your later analysis. Write this statement as though your reader were unfamiliar with the story. Readers will need to know the facts on which you base your arguments and analysis, regardless of their familiarity with the case.

1. *Choose Only Relevant Facts*

Fact patterns often contain more detail than necessary. Present only those facts relevant to your legal and policy analysis and necessary to give your reader a clear picture of what happened. Remember that your analysis will include arguments that you may make, as well as potential arguments for opposing counsel. Thus, the facts underlying both sides' arguments must be included.

2. *Paraphrase*

Use select words or phrases from the record when they capture an idea or convey a concept better than paraphrasing would. Remember, however, that you should control how the facts are presented and must tell a coherent story. Paraphrasing the record and including only select quotes generally result in a clear presentation.

3. *Organize Your Facts Logically*

Do not assume that you should structure your facts in chronological order. You may want to highlight the facts most important to your analysis by beginning with them and then explaining the events that led up to them. Note that the *Bell-Wesley* Statement of Facts, for example, begins with the couple's decision not to have children. It then fills the reader in on the facts leading up to that decision — the three previous pregnancies,

their doctor's advice, etc. (*See* Appendix D, p.137.) This places emphasis on the facts leading to the lawsuit — the Bell-Wesleys had decided not to have children, sought sterilization to insure that, and then had a child. Whether you present your facts in chronological order or not, you can emphasize the most important facts by placing them at the beginning of a paragraph or in separate sentences.

4. *Identify Holes in the Facts*

After analyzing the necessary elements of a cause of action, you may realize that there are holes in the facts. By piecing facts together, you may be able to draw logical inferences. Point out possible inferences as well as gaps in the facts that you have in your Statement of Facts, and remember to address these problems in your Discussion.

5. *Cite to the Record*

When you cite a fact from the record, either through a paraphrase or a direct quote, readers must be able to find it in the record. A good way to reference the record is to use parentheses containing the letter "R." — for "Record" — and the page number on which you found the fact after the sentence in which the fact is cited. If this sentence contained a fact from page eight of the record, for example, it would be referenced as follows: (R.8). (*See* Appendix A, "General Rules of Style and Citation of Authorities," Part I, Section F(3), p.84.)

E. APPLICABLE STATUTES

If the causes of action you have identified are governed by statutes or other regulations, your reader needs to be aware of the relevant parts of the statutes or regulations. You may want to include applicable statutes or regulations in a separate section of the memo. If only a small part of a statute or regulation applies, including that part in the text of your memo or in a footnote may suffice.

F. DISCUSSION

Before writing, you engaged in a long and probably somewhat arduous research process. Coming to terms with legal arguments and opinions can be difficult. The goal of the Discussion section is to make the issues you have struggled with while researching clear to your reader. Present your relevant findings and your analysis of them in a straightforward, detailed, and structured manner. After reading this section, your reader should be familiar with the relevant law on the issues discussed, as well as how and why a court in your jurisdiction is likely to rule on each issue.

1. Where to Begin

Begin by creating some sort of an outline. You will have a number of cases and lots of ideas from your research. Before writing about them, create a structure into which they fit logically. Group relevant cases and arguments together and then decide which group should be discussed first to help your reader understand the issues. If a statute governs your issues, you may want to start by explaining why the statute applies to the facts or by analyzing different elements of a claim. This would entail doing an analysis of the statutory language, backed up by relevant legislative history and cases. In any event, remember that you must present arguments and case law for both sides.

2. Overall Structure

Your arguments should follow logically from one to the next. Remember to use introductory paragraphs and transitions to make your structure clear to your reader.

a. Headings

If you are analyzing different issues on appeal, separate sections for each issue may help your reader follow the logical structure of the discussion. If your arguments are complex, using headings or sub-headings to break down the analysis may be helpful. The *Bell-Wesley* memo uses headings and sub-headings effectively.

Remember to reconsider the Questions Presented. The order of your Questions Presented should follow the order of the answers to those questions in the body of the memo. As you create a structure for the Discussion section, think about how to frame your Questions Presented. If you have preliminary drafts of the Questions Presented, think about how to change their order or content as you gain a better understanding of the issues while working on the Discussion.

b. Paragraph Structure

Lead with conclusions. Just as your entire memo will begin with a summary of your overall conclusions in your Brief Answers section, so should each paragraph begin with a summary statement of the substance of that paragraph. Set forth a conclusion at the beginning of the paragraph, backing it up with the arguments and the case and statutory law that led you to it. Note that this is the opposite of the research process in which you have just engaged. While researching, you started with many facts from many cases and drew conclusions. The reader of your memo should have the luxury of knowing the conclusions first and then reading about the many details that led to them. Your reader should be able to read the first sentence of a paragraph and know exactly what that para-

graph will discuss. (Leading with conclusions may not come naturally at first. Word processors make it very easy to move conclusory sentences from the end of a paragraph to the beginning during the editing process, however.)

Support your conclusions with arguments and cases. After setting forth a conclusion, show the reader why you drew that conclusion by explaining the interpretations of statutes and cases that support it. (*See also* this section, Subsection 3, "Use of Authority," p.37.)

The holding and the relevant facts of each case cited should be clear to the reader. Merely stating the holding, or quoting the court, is inadequate for two reasons. First, without the facts, a holding is just words. Courts may say one thing and do another — showing *how* courts apply a principle to a set of facts is what gives a principle practical meaning. Second, without the facts, it is impossible to determine how the precedent cited may be applied to the facts of the case you are analyzing.

The *Bell-Wesley* memo provides many examples of using detailed analysis of persuasive authority.

> In <u>Hartke v. McKelway</u>, 707 F.2d 1544, 1554 (D.C. Cir. 1983), the United States Court of Appeals for the District of Columbia held that the plaintiff could recover damages for medical costs and pain and suffering, but could not do so for child-rearing expenses. The plaintiff had undergone a tubal ligation, not for economic reasons, but out of fear for her life should she become pregnant again after experiencing an ectopic pregnancy. The court reasoned that it was the pregnancy she sought to avoid through sterilization, not the child; therefore she need be compensated for only the nine months of pregnancy. <u>See also</u> <u>Burke v. Rivo</u>, 551 N.E.2d 1, 5-6 (Mass. 1990) (holding that justification for child-rearing damages lessened where eugenic or therapeutic reasons motivated the desire to avoid birth of a child). In the present case, this reasoning would lead to a decision not to allow damages for child-rearing costs to the Bell-Wesleys. The Bell-Wesleys are not under financial strain, and the primary reason for Scott's sterilization appears to be eugenic. Once a healthy baby was born, the Bell-Wesleys were happy to have him. It is not at all clear that any injury to the Bell-Wesleys extends to the post-conception period.

(*See* Appendix D, p.145.)

Occasionally, citing a case because it contains a relevant standard or principle without going into the facts may be useful. Similarly, using a parenthetical to explain the relevant holding of a case (such as the

parenthetical for *Burke v. Rivo*, above) can be effective when the relevant holding can be summarized briefly and specific comparison of the facts of the case with the one at hand is unnecessary.

Apply the law to the facts at hand. Compare and contrast the facts of the relevant holdings with the facts of your client's potential case. Explain how the facts at hand could lead to a similar outcome, or how certain facts may distinguish your client's case from past cases, leading to a different outcome.

Remember to point out holes in the facts. If a certain cause of action requires facts unknown to you, point that out. Remember also to suggest inferences from the facts you do have.

c. General Notes

Provide background information. Do not assume that your reader knows much about a potential argument. Give a synopsis of the elements required to establish a claim unless you are sure all your potential readers know them.

Explain what you have not done. If you are writing a memo for a long-term project in which others may expand upon your work, you may want to include a paragraph at the end of your Discussion section explaining potential claims you researched and eliminated or areas for further research. You could also create a separate section containing this information. (*See* this part, Section H.) This may facilitate the work of someone coming after you on the same project.

3. Use of Authority

When choosing which cases to cite, select the ones with the greatest relevance (the ones that are most nearly "on point") and the greatest weight, based on their sources. If you find cases in your jurisdiction that are on point, they provide binding authority. That is, judges, following the principle of stare decisis, must follow them, unless convinced that they are distinguishable. Because many moot court cases are set in mythical jurisdictions and are cases of first impression, you may well find no binding authority. You must rely instead on persuasive authority — cases that are on point but are from different jurisdictions. Opinions of the Supreme Court of the United States, a federal circuit court, or a state court of last resort are the most persuasive sources. You may also cite a variety of jurisdictions to indicate that a given proposition is widely accepted. In this situation, of course, three cases from three states will be more effective than three cases from one state. If no cases from any jurisdiction are

directly on point, analogize to cases from related subject areas. Explain to the court why the animating force (which you must identify for the court) behind those cases mandates a similar holding in yours.

Uncontested propositions of law, such as the definition of negligence, rarely require more than one authority in a citation.

G. CONCLUSION

Include a brief summary of your conclusions in this section similar to, though not identical to, your Brief Answers (your reader can always look at your Brief Answers again; this is an opportunity to present your conclusions in a new way). As in the Brief Answers, do not cite authorities here — merely set forth your conclusions.

H. SCOPE OF RESEARCH

In order to allow others to pick up where you left off and not to retrace your research steps, use this section to list the topics under which you searched and the sources you consulted. Explain how you searched and suggest ideas for further searches, if you have them. Knowing what you have done may allow your reader to suggest additional resources.

IV.   Sample Memorandum: *Bell-Wesley v. O'Toole*

A sample memo evaluating potential arguments for the Bell-Wesleys on appeal to the Ames Supreme Court is located in Appendix D. The memorandum evaluates the status of wrongful pregnancy as a cause of action; presents the policy and case law arguments on both sides; and suggests ways in which the Bell-Wesleys' case could be argued on appeal.

CHAPTER 4
Writing a Brief

I.   Introduction

A. THE PURPOSE OF A BRIEF

An advocate almost always submits her case to a court in written form. In appellate courts, these documents are called briefs. In trial courts, these are sometimes called memoranda of law; a litigant might entitle one "Memorandum in Support of the Defendant's Motion for Summary Judgment." These documents differ from the legal research memoranda described in Chapter 3, which summarize and analyze the law in a particular area, but which are not presented to a court. To avoid confusion, this chapter uses the term "brief." The sample briefs in *Bell-Wesley v. O'Toole* in Appendix E are written for submission to the Supreme Court of the State of Ames, an appellate court. The same principles apply, however, to documents submitted to lower courts.

A brief presents the advocate's view of the strongest arguments, authority, and background material in a case. The brief aids the court in rendering its decision. A brief gives each side an opportunity to describe its position clearly, accurately, and assertively to the court. A strong brief compels the court to rule in favor of the writer. A strong brief is also complete and reliable. Judges often rely on briefs as the foundation for their decision-making and as a resource for writing an opinion.

B. STYLE

Good brief writing builds on the skills of good writing. The same challenges of imagination, phrasing, and structure must be met. Nonetheless, a brief is a persuasive piece of writing; and each element of it should be geared toward convincing the court to decide in your favor.

A brief should be simple, well-organized, interesting, complete, and reliable. Within those constraints, however, a writer has discretion in selecting writing style. Opinions differ over what tone is the most persuasive. Some advocates are dispassionate, while others are more aggressive and adversarial.

Some basic principles should be applied:

- Strategically select every word by analyzing its tactical value. For example, even choosing the names of the parties in the case can be significant. The overuse of "appellant" and "appellee" in a brief can be confusing to a reader who does not share your intimate understanding of the record. Instead, you should characterize the parties in a manner that will influence the reader's perception of them. For instance, you might try to evoke the reader's sympathy for the client by using a personal title and using a more formal title for the adversary. Regardless of the route, you should be consistent throughout the brief.

- Use action verbs. A forceful argument uses action verbs, rather than only forms of the verb "to be." On the other hand, damaging facts and arguments may be downplayed by using the passive voice.

- Avoid complex language, including "legalese."

- Avoid extended quotations. Short quotations can be used to add variety or emphasis. If there is no concise quotation, a paraphrase with a citation may still be better. An impatient reader will skip lengthy quotations. Explain the relevance of the quotation; do not expect the court to figure out how it applies to your case.

C. COMPARING BRIEF WRITING AND ORAL ADVOCACY

The brief and the oral argument each have strengths and weaknesses as tools of persuasion and as means of conveying information. Citations, numbers, and dates belong in a brief because they are most easily absorbed visually. A brief should contain all the information necessary for the court to reach a decision. By contrast, everything in a brief will not be in an oral argument. The oral argument is similar to a conversation with the court, providing an opportunity to give the court an overall impression of the case and to answer lingering questions. A successful advocate will recognize the strategic values of the brief and the oral argument and exploit the strengths of each.

D. CONVENTION

Brief writers follow different patterns. There is no set formula for a brief, but there are recognized conventions. This is not surprising, since writers of briefs have similar training and the common goal of persuasion. Sometimes there are formal constraints on the brief writer. An attorney always consults the rules of his or her jurisdiction. The courts may proscribe length, the parts, and other requirements for the brief. Beginning brief writers might choose to follow traditional patterns. Form will inspire confidence; individual preferences will develop with experience.

Creativity, particularly in the arguments, is important, but it is best employed within the confines set by common practice. To this end, this chapter presents the common practice.

E. EDITING

Some writers say that there is no good writing, only good rewriting. Certain word patterns can invariably be eliminated, without any loss of meaning. The following are examples of such terms: "It can be argued," "It seems that," "Cases have clearly held," and "It is beyond argument that." Without such phrases, prose is much clearer, stronger, and more direct. To bolster your credibility, eliminate adverbs and adjectives where nouns and verbs will convey the same points. Be careful about typographical errors; careless mistakes compromise your credibility. Good form and attention to detail inspire the court's confidence in your research and analysis.

II.   Parts of a Brief

A brief consists of various parts, each designed to convey a specific type of information. While brief writers sometimes add or omit parts, most briefs contain these sections:

A.   Questions Presented;

B.   Introduction;

C.   Statement of Facts;

D.   Argument; and

E.   Conclusion.

A. QUESTIONS PRESENTED

First, the brief must set the agenda for the court by presenting the questions that should be answered in order to decide the case. The function of the Questions Presented in the brief is similar to their function in the legal research memorandum. Unlike those in the memorandum, however, the Questions Presented in the brief aim to persuade. They must balance advocacy and accuracy. A judge's initial reaction to the merit of the motion or appeal is often based upon this formulation of what the counsel considers to be vital to her case. Like the brief as a whole, the questions must be simple, interesting, complete, and reliable. (For a discussion of the function of Questions Presented in a legal memorandum, see Chapter 3, "Writing a Legal Research Memorandum," Part III, Section B, p.31.)

Crafting the Questions Presented is a useful exercise with which to begin writing the brief because it forces the writer to frame and clarify the key issues. Some brief writers, however, prefer to save this task for last, after they have articulated their argument in detail. Others go back and

forth. Either way, writing and rewriting the questions takes a great deal of time. The Questions Presented create the first impression of each side's version of the case.

1. How Many?

The number of Questions Presented depends upon the number of arguments an advocate decides to make. Each question and argument should relate to the core theory. (For a discussion of core theory, see Chapter 1, "Interpreting Facts and Developing Core Theory," Part II, p.3). Avoid weakening strong points by associating them with less momentous arguments. These considerations, in conjunction with space restrictions set by court rule or assignment, will probably leave two, three, or in rare instances, four arguments in your brief.

2. Structure

The Questions Presented are usually placed at the beginning of the text. They should be in the order in which their corresponding arguments appear in the brief. Each question should be independent and require no reference to any point contained in a previous question. Although an argument may be complex, an advocate should try to craft clear and easy-to-read questions. Questions with many subclauses tend to get convoluted.

3. Substance

The questions should suggest answers the writer wants the court to reach. To achieve this, questions should mesh important facts with the law the writer wants the court to apply. This enables a litigant to impart some of the flavor of the argument to the reader from the very start. Fact-filled questions are always more useful than abstract questions of law.

A litigant should avoid assuming the issue in dispute. For example, the question "Does an unreasonable search violate the Fourth Amendment?" assumes that the search in question was unreasonable. This question is poorly crafted, because the real issue is whether the particular search in the case was an unreasonable search. There is no question that if the search were unreasonable, it would violate the Fourth Amendment.

The Questions Presented should serve as signposts for the arguments. They should plant the first seeds of persuasion. A reader should always be able to tell which side wrote a brief simply by reading the Questions Presented. An effective Question Presented indicates that the court can reasonably rule in only one way. Be careful, however, not to irritate the court with overly biased questions that suggest by their stridency the inevitable counter-argument.

The Questions Presented should be answerable by either a "yes" or a "no." For purpose of symmetry, try to frame all of the questions in a brief so that they are answered the same way, either all "yes" or all "no," in support of your position.

4. Examples

Different advocates arguing *Bell-Wesley v. O'Toole* might draft the following Questions Presented:

> 1. Is a doctor who negligently performs a vasectomy liable for the costs of raising a child when the husband subsequently impregnates his wife and they have an unplanned baby?

> 2. Where a couple, after having several congenitally deformed children who died soon after birth, has a child conceived after an unsuccessfully performed vasectomy, and refused to abort, or give the child up for adoption, should the doctor who performed the vasectomy be held liable for all the costs of raising that child when the couple could well afford to have the child, and benefited from the doctor's negligence by receiving the healthy child that they had always wanted?

> 3. Should a doctor whose negligent performance of a sterilization inflicted numerous injuries upon a couple be held responsible for the full extent of his negligence by requiring him to compensate the couple for the medical costs, the physical and emotional pain and suffering, and the extensive financial costs associated with raising a child?

The most effective question is the third one. It suggests the answer the litigant wants the court to reach, "yes." It incorporates facts of the case, such as the suffering of the couple. The choice of words and phrases like "inflicted," "full extent of his negligence," and "extensive" set the tone for the subsequent argument. It also includes the legal issues, negligence and damages.

By contrast, the first question is not strong enough. The reader cannot tell which side the author represents. The use of "negligently" suggests she represents the couple, but the word "unplanned" is not favorable to the couple. The author does not lead the reader to any answer. Few facts are incorporated into the question. While a brief writer should strive for clear and concise Questions Presented, this question is incomplete.

Complicated and difficult to follow, Question 2 errs the other way. Although it is clear the writer represents the doctor, the author uses too many clauses. While certain phrases, like "the healthy child that they had always wanted," show promise, they are lost in the complexity of the question.

Avoid confusing questions, like Question 2, and simplistic questions, like Question 1. Instead, seek a middle ground, as in Question 3. (For examples of effective Questions Presented, see the sample briefs in *Bell-Wesley v. O'Toole* in Appendix E, pp.160, 178.)

B. INTRODUCTION

A one-paragraph road map of the essential facts and the course of the advocate's arguments may be useful to judges, particularly in complex cases. A good Introduction is clear and concise, and contains no citations. You might use the Introduction to acquaint the reader with the core theory. For example, the attorney for the Bell-Wesleys used an Introduction to stress their view that Dr. O'Toole's negligence should not be excused simply because one of the products of his negligence was a child. (*See* Appendix E, p.160.) Rules governing the location of an Introduction vary by jurisdiction.

C. STATEMENT OF FACTS

The Statement of Facts tells one side's view as to what happened in the "real world" to bring this case into court. For example, each side in *Bell-Wesley v. O'Toole* informs the court about the couple's decision that Scott would have a vasectomy:

The attorney for the Bell-Wesleys writes:

> Rebecca and Scott Bell-Wesley made a conscious decision to forego having children. (R.1) Three of their children died in infancy due to congenital defects. (R.1) Their doctor, Dr. Stephen O'Toole, informed them that there was a seventy-five percent probability that any child they conceived would suffer from the same congenital deformity. Given their previous failures, the information from their doctor, and a fear of bringing a deformed child into the world, Rebecca and Scott Bell-Wesley chose to remain childless. (R.1,11) They did not adopt. Instead, they elected to devote their lives to each other and to their occupations.

(*See* Appendix E, p.161.)

In contrast, the attorney for Dr. O'Toole writes:

> On three occasions before the January 1996 birth of their son, Frank Michael Bell, the Bell-Wesleys had attempted to start a family. (R.1) Each time, however, Mrs. Bell-Wesley gave birth to a congenitally deformed infant that died within six months. (R.1) Dr. O'Toole informed the Bell-Wesleys that there was a seventy-five percent chance that any child they conceived

```
          would suffer the same deformity. (R.1)  For the
          sole purpose of avoiding the conception of
          another deformed child, the Bell-Wesleys decided
          to have Dr. O'Toole sterilize Mr. Bell-Wesley.
          (R.7)
```

(*See* Appendix E, p.178.)

Both sides describe the same facts using very different language. The Bell-Wesleys stress the "conscious decision to forego having children," while Dr. O'Toole emphasizes that the "sole purpose" of the decision was to avoid the "conception of another deformed child." In parentheses, the authors cite to the Record in the case.

The subjective Statement of Facts in the brief differs from the objective Statement of Facts in the legal memorandum. (For a discussion of the Statement of Facts in a legal memorandum, see Chapter 3, "Writing a Legal Research Memorandum," Part III, Section D, p.33.) Nonetheless, while the Statement of Facts in each sample brief tells the story from a different perspective, neither crosses the line into drawing unsupported conclusions, exaggerating, or making legal arguments.

Both sides must present a complete and reliable, yet simple and interesting, version of the facts of the case. Those facts are the material from which you create arguments, but to some judges a fair, yet persuasive, Statement of Facts can be more dispositive than a carefully crafted Argument. After reading your Statement of Facts, the judge should want to interpret the law in your favor.

1. Identifying the Facts

Facts can be divided into two categories — substantive and procedural. Substantive facts describe events that happened before the litigation and, in appellate briefs, at trial. Procedural facts describe the legal path that the case has taken up to the point of the brief. Advocates may present these two types of facts separately. For example, they might title this section of their brief, "Statement of the Case," and under this section have two subheadings entitled, "Proceedings Below" or "Procedural History" and "Statement of Facts." Some appellate courts require this separation. In many courts, both types of facts may be combined in a general Statement of the Case. Regardless of how substantive and procedural facts are organized, both must be included.

2. Choosing the Facts

Separate the relevant facts from the irrelevant ones in the record. A litigant who omits the most relevant facts supporting her opponent's position is likely to impair her credibility. A good Statement of the Facts will do more than just summarize the record; it will shape the facts into a narrative that interests the reader and favors the author's position.

3. *Using the Record*

Use only the facts found in the record or facts of general knowledge, which are subject to "judicial notice." You can use admissions by the other side as positive proof of a fact considered material.

The creativity you demonstrate in presenting a persuasive fact must not, however, extend to fabricating or exaggerating information. A judge will not let a fabricated "fact" slide by as a clever inference. All assumptions of fact must be firmly grounded in the record. (For examples of citations to the record, see the Statements of Facts in the sample briefs for *Bell-Wesley v. O'Toole* in Appendix E.) Certain undeniable assertions, however, such as the fact that apples do not fall up, can be used without appearing in the record. Other information, like the conclusions of relevant sociological studies, can be used even though they are not part of the record as long as proper authority is cited.

Holes in the record are not necessarily useless. You can successfully use "negative facts" to buttress your position. Negative facts are facts that the other side can neither establish nor disprove, because they do not exist in the record. You can effectively use negative facts to create a gap of essential knowledge, requiring a ruling in your client's favor. For example, a defendant-appellee may show that the plaintiff-appellant never met his burden of proof by pointing to the absence in the record of facts indicating otherwise. You can also make inferences from what is missing from the record. For example, the *Bell-Wesley v. O'Toole* record is silent on the issue of whether Scott and Rebecca ever considered adopting a child after learning that there was a high likelihood that any child they conceived would suffer a congenital birth defect. Nonetheless, in the appellants' Statement of the Case, there is an inference:

```
Rebecca  and  Scott  Bell-Wesley  chose  to  remain
childless.(R.1) They did not adopt.  Instead, they
elected to devote their lives to each other and to
their occupations.
```

(*See* Appendix E, p.161.) Do not be afraid to make effective use of holes in the record.

(For a thorough consideration of the use of the record, see Chapter 1, "Interpreting Facts and Developing Core Theory.")

4. *Organizing the Facts*

The organization of the facts is critical. How the judge views the facts will influence how she views the case. Every word in the Statement of Facts should be geared toward making the brief a better instrument of persuasion or a more complete and reliable resource. A chronological narrative may or may not be the most persuasive structure for telling the story. Starting with the conflict or injury, and later describing what preceded it, may be the most compelling way to begin. Some points should be remembered.

- Use labels that will appropriately characterize the parties.

- Use words with effective connotations.

- Never assume the reader has any prior knowledge of the case. Introduce the characters. Avoid abbreviations with which the court may not be familiar.

5. *Handling Adverse Facts*

Reliability is essential. Glaring omissions of adverse facts central to the other side's case will decrease credibility with the court. The negative side of the case will appear less damaging if cautiously disclosed in the Statement of Facts.

Unfavorable facts which must be included should be downplayed. Passive verbs can dilute the force of such statements. Damaging material can be placed in subordinate clauses. Once a harmful fact is mentioned, there is no need to emphasize it. For example, while an appellant needs to disclose that there was an adverse judgment below, he or she need not disclose that the district judge rejected each and every contention. Rest assured that the appellee will mention that. For example, in *Bell-Wesley v. O'Toole*, the doctor's attorney referred to his client's negligence by saying Dr. O'Toole "performed a vasectomy" and "mistakenly informed" Mr. Bell-Wesley that he was sterile. (*See* Appendix E, p.179.) On the other hand, the Bell-Wesleys' attorney characterized the same acts as "repeated acts of negligence" in performing both the vasectomy and the sperm count. (*See* Appendix E, p.163.)

6. *Separating Fact From Argument*

The desire to paint a persuasive factual picture should not cross the boundary into argument. You risk losing credibility if you slant the facts too much. The facts should tell the story by themselves. They are used to support conclusions; they must not be expressed as conclusions. For example, a fact statement should not contain conclusions of law, such as "the defendant was negligent." Instead, explain what the defendant did, allowing the court to reach its own conclusion that the defendant acted negligently. The court should be left to draw the legal conclusion once you have provided the factual foundation. The Statement of Facts should make the appropriate conclusions obvious. (One exception to this rule is that you may report the conclusions of law of the lower court(s) in a Statement of Facts for an appellate brief. *See, e.g.,* Appendix E, p.163.)

D. ARGUMENT

The arguments comprise the body of the brief. After considering legal precedent, policy, and the facts of the case, choose the strongest arguments. Discard weaker or less clear arguments because including them

might dilute the force of the main points. Buttress the arguments with authority. Anticipate, preempt, or rebut the opponent's crucial arguments and distinguish opposing cases.

1. Argument Headings

Each argument begins with a complete sentence called an "argument heading." The heading should be a concise summary of the argument. The heading identifies the specific portion of the argument to be advanced in that section of the brief. Some attorneys craft the argument headings to mirror the Questions Presented in phrasing and structure. In any event, the argument headings should state affirmatively the resolution of the issues raised in the Questions Presented. An effective argument heading will identify the applicable law; the way in which the law applies to the facts of the case; and the conclusion that follows from that application. Not every relevant legal or factual issue can fit in a heading. Adjectives and adverbs should not be used to exaggerate the argument. Argument headings are conventionally in capital letters and single spaced.

2. Subheadings

Subheadings may be used to partition arguments, especially complex ones. When an argument is relatively simple, however, subheadings may interrupt the flow of the argument. Subheadings are generally in lower case, with initial capitals, and are underscored.

An example of an argument heading and subheadings from the sample brief for Dr. O'Toole follows:

I.   THIS COURT SHOULD NOT AWARD THE BELL-WESLEYS
        DAMAGES FOR THE COSTS OF RAISING THEIR NORMAL,
        HEALTHY SON TO MAJORITY.

        A.   Frank's Birth Did Not Injure the
                Bell-Wesleys, Because They Sought
                Sterilization for Non-Economic
                Reasons.

        B.   Awarding Full Child-Rearing Costs Harms
                the Mental Health of Unwanted Children,
                Discourages Doctors From Performing
                Needed Sterilizations, and Grants
                Windfalls to Parents.

(*See* Appendix E, p.175.) This argument heading identifies the legal issue of damages. It also describes how the law relates to the facts of the case: *because* the Bell-Wesleys sought sterilization for non-economic reasons, they suffered no legally cognizable injury. Furthermore, it neatly breaks the main argument down into its legal and policy components. Finally, the argument heading and subheadings are not bolstered by unnecessary adverbs or adjectives.

3. Standard of Review

An appellate brief should indicate the standard of review. The standard of review dictates how an appeals court must treat the findings of a lower court. Generally, an appeals court must defer to a trial court's findings of fact, disturbing them only if they are "clearly erroneous." An appeals court may make its own determinations on the law, regardless of the trial court decision. This is called "de novo" review. The distinction between fact and law, however, is not always easily discernible.

You should research the standard of review for the particular cause of action involved.   A case from the appropriate jurisdiction will usually clarify the standard of review. For example, in some contract cases, an appellate judge may make new findings on the interpretation of a contract term, but she should defer to the trial judge's assessment of oral testimony.

If it is contentious, then the "correct" standard of review should be argued along with the other points. The standard of review may be included in the first paragraph of the first argument. Alternatively, it may be placed in a separate section between the Statement of Facts and the Argument. In some instances, you will want to present the standard of review in an argument subheading. The prominence of the standard of review in a brief will depend on how favorable it is to your side. Thus, this essential part of an appellate brief can also provide a strategic advantage.

You may choose to argue using the standard of review throughout the brief. For example, you may frame the Questions Presented or argument headings in light of the standard of review. The attorney for the appellee who won in the trial court will stress the "clearly erroneous" element. The appellant, however, will emphasize that no deference should be given to the trial court's interpretation of the law.

Examples of how the attorneys in *Bell-Wesley v. O'Toole* used the standard of review follow:

The Bell-Wesleys' brief:

> These foreseeable damages include the costs of
> having and raising their unwanted child. The
> trial court's denial of the Bell-Wesleys' prayer
> for compensation for the expense of raising the
> unwanted child is a finding of law that can and
> should be overturned. See Sherlock v. Stillwater
> Clinic, 260 N.W.2d 169, 172 (Minn. 1977) (noting
> that decisions of law are reviewed de novo).

(*See* Appendix E, p.163.)

Dr. O'Toole's brief:

> While this court may review issues of law de
> novo, it must defer to the trial court's findings
> of fact. See Sherlock v. Stillwater Clinic, 260
> N.W.2d 169, 172 (Minn. 1977) (deferring to trial
> court determination of facts to support a
> negligence decision).

(*See* Appendix E, p.180.)

The attorney for the appellants, the Bell-Wesleys, stresses that the appellate court need not follow the trial court's refusal to recognize a cause of action for wrongful birth. The attorney for the appellee, Dr. O'Toole, downplays, but nonetheless includes the standard of review for legal findings. He emphasizes the need to follow the lower court's findings of fact.

4. *Organization and Structure of Arguments*

Brief writers often place the strongest arguments first. Many attorneys write arguments in the pattern of a logical syllogism. The Argument might contain, after the argument heading:

- Introductory statement of the legal standard, framed in terms of this case, and giving the conclusion up front;

- Application of the legal standard to the facts of the case;

- Summary;

- Rebuttal; and

- Conclusion stating what you have shown.

An effective approach to organization is to make the *first* sentence of each paragraph a *"conclusion"* that tells the reader what will be argued in that paragraph. A good test of the logical structure and cohesiveness of your brief is to read the first sentence of each paragraph. This scan should summarize the facts and argument. This enables a judge to review the brief selectively, closely reading some paragraphs (probably the more controversial ones) while skimming others.

5. *Substance of the Argument*

The argument should muster facts and law to persuade the court to rule in one side's favor. Never view the Statement of Facts section as the only place for the facts. Do not devote long sections of the brief, for example, to the historical evolution of a current legal standard. This style is simply not persuasive. Direct references to the facts of the case are essential ingredients of the arguments, because the court must apply principles of law to the particular facts of the case. A skillful brief writer will attempt to incorporate facts into every paragraph of the argument.

Still, you cannot make unsupported assertions, and you must provide the cases, precedent, and authorities that give the court the tools to reach a particular decision. However, these tools will be closely related to the facts. Successful arguments depend on integration of facts and law.

Identify elements of cases favorable to your side and tie those elements into the facts of the present case. A particularly favorable case may be discussed at greater length. A particularly unfavorable case may need to be distinguished.

Many attorneys make what are broadly called "public policy" arguments. These may be the most compelling arguments in a brief. Roughly speaking, any argument that the outcome benefits the public interest falls into this category. Some brief writers place public policy arguments under separate headings. Often, however, they appear in a separate paragraph under a particular argument heading. For example, the attorney for Dr. O'Toole makes a public policy argument about the effect of awarding full damages. He writes, "[a]warding full child-rearing costs might cause Frank severe emotional trauma." (*See* Appendix E, p.183.) Furthermore, according to the writer, deciding in Dr. O'Toole's favor furthers the public policy against unreasonable liability for physicians. Public policy informs most opinions. When analyzing and interpreting precedents, try to determine what policy rationales underlie them.

An advocate who urges a change or modification of the law as it has developed in cases may want to include references to scholars or other authorities that have also argued for such a change. This may make the court more "comfortable" with departing from precedent or navigating uncharted territory. (For examples of uses of law review articles, see the sample briefs in Appendix E.)

6. *Rebuttal and Preemption of Arguments*

A brief may respond to the opponent's arguments. Evading or concealing the difficult points on your side may leave their resolution to the court, without your guidance. You can try to show the illogic of the opponent's argument; demonstrate how the facts fail to support the legal conclusion; and point out the unfortunate consequences that would flow from a decision for the other side. A brief might address the other side's argument as part of the affirmative presentation of the case, attacking the opponent's arguments by directly confronting them. Regardless, the tone of each brief must remain affirmative and not convey a defensive posture. Blanket statements characterizing the other side as wrong are useless and may detract from your credibility.

The brief should not summarize the other side's arguments. This wastes space and puts the writer in a purely defensive position. You should counter the other side's arguments but should not make the arguments for the other side.

A respondent or appellee should use any opportunity to review the brief of the moving party, or appellant, before she files her own brief. Because the time between filings is usually short, the respondent will have already researched and prepared arguments. The respondent should highlight weaknesses of the moving party's argument. Still, a point-by-point refutation is rarely the ideal format for a respondent's brief. Independent arguments are stronger and more persuasive.

7. *Arguing in the Alternative*

For some legal arguments there are "fall-back" positions. If the court fails to agree with one side's main position, the court can turn to the advocate's alternative argument. For example, in *Bell-Wesley*, the Bell-Wesleys' attorney makes alternative arguments. She argues that based on the law and facts, the Bell-Wesleys should receive full child-rearing damages. In the alternative, she argues that if the court does not award full child-rearing damages, the court should award full recovery offset by the emotional benefits the Bell-Wesleys receive from Frank. (*See* Appendix E, p.158.)

Arguing in the alternative should never force you to compromise your core theory. If an alternative argument contradicts your core theory, you might choose to omit it from the brief, but reserve it for oral argument. If the judges appear to disfavor the main argument, then raise the alternative one.

E. CONCLUSION

The brief should end with a section entitled, "Conclusion," which states the remedy or relief sought. A summary is usually *unhelpful* here. It may be difficult to determine which components of an argument a court will find persuasive. Therefore, emphasizing one or the other in summary may undermine the persuasive effect of the winning argument. Also, page limits may require leaving out details, and it may be better to omit a recapitulation of arguments than a useful authority or a paragraph of the Argument. Still, a brief summary may be effective if it evokes the core theory.

III. Use of Authority

When properly used, authorities aid in convincing the reader to adopt the propositions asserted. The authorities with the greatest relevance (those most "on point") and the greatest weight should be cited. The most relevant are usually those with similar facts. Decisions that bind the particular court have the greatest weight. Citing a variety of jurisdictions, however, shows that courts widely accept a proposition. Uncontested propositions of law, such as the definition of negligence, rarely require more than one authority in a citation. Nothing is gained from merely stringing citations together.

A. USE OF PARENTHETICALS

While major cases should be discussed at more length, others can sometimes be effectively summarized by using parentheticals. In some instances the most effective way to use a case is to paraphrase the principle it stands for and follow that with a citation. An unelaborated or "bare" cite, giving only the case name and the reporter, will not help the court. Parentheticals, abstracting the facts of the case and/or quoting critical language, aid the reader by explaining the relevance, similarity, or difference of the cited case to the case at hand. (*See* Appendix A, "General Rules of Style and Citation of Authorities," Part III, Section C, p.92.)

There are many examples of parentheticals in the sample briefs. They include:

> Hartke v. McKelway, 707 F.2d 1544, 1555 (D.C. Cir. 1983) (holding that mother's anxiety about unborn child's potential deformity merited damage award), cert. denied, 464 U.S. 983 (1983).

(*See* Appendix E, p.165.)

> See, e.g., Wilbur v. Kerr, 628 S.W.2d 568, 571
> (Ark. 1982) (denying recovery for the expense of
> raising an unwanted, healthy child).

(*See* Appendix E, p.183.)

Do not overuse parentheticals. Particularly important cases generally need more extensive treatment than a parenthetical provides. The best cases may be discussed at length. An advocate might include a paragraph explaining how the legal principle in a precedent governs the issue before the court, or why it must be distinguished. In either situation, the facts of the case before the court should be emphasized for their similarities and/or differences to the facts of the precedent.

B. CONTRARY AUTHORITY

For the sake of reliability and completeness, you should cite important cases standing *against* the propositions advanced in the brief. The ethical rules of most jurisdictions require citation of contrary authority. You can distinguish these cases, either in the text or in a parenthetical, by undermining their logic or showing differences in the facts. When cited as adverse to the proposition raised, a contrary authority should be signaled with "*But see.*" Citation of contrary authority shows thoroughness and may negate damage done by the adverse cases.

IV.   Formalities

A. TITLE PAGE

A title page provides the relevant information about the case: the court, the docket number, the names of the parties, the names of the attorneys, and the date and place of hearing.

A full designation of the parties (e.g., "Plaintiff-Appellant") should appear on the title page, but need not be repeated elsewhere in the brief. In most state jurisdictions and lower federal courts, the original order of the parties is maintained in the case on appeal. The Supreme Court of the United States names the appealing party first.

Counsels' names, formal title (e.g., "Attorney for the Appellee"), and the date and place of the oral argument are placed in the lower right hand corner. (For examples of title pages, see the sample briefs in Appendix E, pp.157, 174.)

B. TABLE OF CONTENTS

The Table of Contents should list the components of the brief, including Statement of the Case or Statement of Facts, Argument (headings and subheadings), and the Conclusion, along with the page number on which each can be found. (For examples of Tables of Contents, see the sample briefs in Appendix E, pp.158, 175.)

C. TABLE OF CITATIONS

Here the writer lists all of the authorities used and indicates where they are cited in the brief. The Table of Citations or Table of Authorities, demands great technical care. Citations must be accurate and complete, and must include all of the information required by *The Bluebook*. All page numbers, volume numbers, underlining, parentheses, brackets, and spacing should be checked carefully. (For examples of Tables of Citations, see the sample briefs in Appendix E, pp.159, 176.)

The list of citations may be divided into at least three sections: "Cases," "Statutes," and "Miscellaneous." Entries should be arranged alphabetically within each category. "Miscellaneous" can be subdivided into "Restatements," "Treatises," etc., if need be.

V.   Sample Briefs: *Bell-Wesley v. O'Toole*

Sample briefs for both parties in the case of *Bell-Wesley v. O'Toole* appear in Appendix E.

As you know from reading the sample Record, this case involves a wrongful pregnancy action. On appeal, the legal issue is whether or not the Bell-Wesleys should receive damages for the costs of raising their son Frank, who was born after Dr. O'Toole negligently performed a vasectomy and sperm count.

The brief for Dr. O'Toole argues that the Bell-Wesleys should not receive any child-rearing costs. It cites supportive legal authority, stressing that the reason the Bell-Wesleys obtained sterilization, to avoid the birth of another deformed baby, means they cannot recover for any costs beyond the pre-natal period. It also reviews public policy reasons for this position. The attorney for Dr. O'Toole recognizes, however, that the Bell-Wesleys will argue that they should receive full costs, but that the court could still apply the equitable "benefit rule" to offset damages by the benefit the Bell-Wesleys receive from Frank. Therefore, the brief for Dr. O'Toole contests that the "benefit rule" is inapplicable when the intangible benefits of a child are involved. Nonetheless, the writer maintains that even if the court adopts the "benefit rule," it should nonetheless find that the benefit to the Bell-Wesleys outweighs the costs. Note also the close comparison of Hartke v. McElway with the facts of the Bell-Wesleys' case in the brief for Dr. O'Toole. (*See* Appendix E, p.181).

The brief for the Bell-Wesleys argues that they should receive all damages flowing naturally from the negligence of Dr. O'Toole. Their side has far less case authority, but many convincing policy arguments. The Bell-Wesleys also argue in the alternative that if the judge refuses to award full damages because of the benefit bestowed on them through a healthy child, the judge should apply the benefit rule (providing them with full recovery less the amount of the benefit they derive from the child).

Finally, note that the two sides handle the term "benefit rule" differently. Perhaps because he wishes to cast doubt on the applicability of the benefit rule to wrongful pregnancy actions, Dr. O'Toole's attorney consistently sets the term off with quotation marks. Stratagems like these can play a vital role in the effectiveness of your briefs.

CHAPTER 5

Oral Argument

Oral argument is frequently the culmination of your efforts as an advocate. It is used most often in appellate litigation and in certain phases of lower court litigation, such as summary judgment motions; however, the bulk of pre-trial and trial briefs are not supplemented by oral argument. Nonetheless, the in-court argument is an historic part of American advocacy. In the early years of the Supreme Court, arguments lasted for hours, if not days. Although caseload pressures have made modern courts reduce the time available to argue cases, sometimes to twenty or thirty minutes, oral argument presents a valuable opportunity to convince the court of the merits of your case and to dispel any doubts particular judges may have after reading the briefs.

Effective oral persuasion is in many ways different from brief writing. It is an interactive effort requiring spontaneous responses to the judges' questions, as well as a clear initial presentation of the case. It takes place under strict time limits, so that the advocate must prioritize arguments even more radically than in the brief. Finally, the effectiveness of oral argument depends on the attorney's physical presence and speaking style. The oral argument is a logical extension of the brief, building on its foundations. If you are prepared to defend your core theory and are familiar with the supporting case law, you will be able to answer the judges' questions confidently. As in brief writing, diverse styles and approaches may be equally successful. There is no one right way to frame an oral argument.

In appellate litigation, our model for this chapter, the structure of an oral argument is simple and direct. The appellant (or "petitioner") rises first to introduce the facts of the case, and then to explain why the court should reverse the lower tribunal's decision. The appellee (or "respondent") then argues her side of the case, defending the lower court's decision. Finally, the appellant may rebut her opponent's assertions. Throughout the argument the judges are likely to interrupt counsels' presentations with questions. Attention to the judges' concerns, and creative responses to any hypotheticals they may pose, are often the most important aspects of a good oral argument.

I.   Preparing for Oral Argument

Preparation for oral argument should focus on both substance and style. Careful study of the facts, the relevant authorities, and the arguments will enable you to defend your brief and to answer questions adequately. Rehearsing the argument is also important, in order to become comfortable with public speaking and to choose the best ways of phrasing arguments. You should prepare to stay focused (developing a consistent argument; making sure not to be distracted or trapped by leading questions; and speaking so as to emphasize the key points). At the same time, you should also prepare to be flexible (inventing responses on the spot when necessary and being sensitive to the personalities and concerns of judges and opposing counsel).

The following is a step-by-step outline of basic techniques for preparing for oral argument.

A. STUDY THE RECORD AND AUTHORITIES

Success in oral argument requires detailed knowledge of the record and the briefs. As the court's decision ultimately turns on the facts, it is important to understand — and have an identifiable point of view on — the events giving rise to the cause of action and the facts and issues discussed in the lower court's opinion. References to the record will likely enhance the court's confidence in other aspects of the argument; incomplete knowledge of the record can be very damaging.

Studying the cases included in both sides' briefs is necessary because judges often use the oral argument to determine which case precedents should guide the decision, and to determine whether the parties' arguments based on precedent are consistent. You should prepare to analogize your case to helpful precedents and distinguish harmful ones. Writing short case abstracts and indexing the record may be helpful both in the study phase and to ensure easy reference during the argument. However, an advocate who can discuss the cases and facts without referring to notes may be able to have a more natural dialogue with the judge, and therefore, may be more successful.

Preparation should address authorities raised in the other party's brief. In addition, new arguments that were not presented in your own brief sometimes may be raised orally before the court (although court rules may restrict the use of cases not cited in the brief). You may use this opportunity to correct what judges perceive as ambiguities or flaws in the original brief.

B. ANALYZE THE ARGUMENTS

To make strategic decisions regarding the arguments most amenable to oral presentation, the advocate should make a methodical attempt to break down the arguments presented in her own and the opponent's briefs. Together with knowledge of the record and authorities, a fresh look at the arguments will give a complete background against which to make strategic and tactical choices concerning both substance and style. Often the most successful oral arguments have a public policy keynote or are very simple, although certain kinds of cases (such as those based on statutory or rule interpretation) may depend on relatively technical points. Choosing effective arguments for oral presentation often means separating the wheat from the chaff of an argument. Although there may be many reasons to find for your client, your job is to emphasize what you see as the most important reasons, or those that may have the most influence on future cases. The following guidelines can aid you in selecting and refining arguments.

1. Use a Core Theory

The demands of oral argument illustrate the importance of having a pithy, convincing core theory — a one or two sentence explanation of the essence of a party's position. (For a complete description of core theory, see Chapter 1, "Interpreting Facts and Developing Core Theory," Part II, p.3.) Both a good brief and a good oral argument will stress one central theme, and approach that theme from different angles — facts, law, policy. Yet in oral argument, the advocate should be prepared to express the core theory even more simply and memorably than in the brief. Some attorneys' experiences indicate that policy arguments play a larger role in supporting core theory in oral argument than in the brief.

When organizing the argument, keep in mind the relationship between each assertion and the core theory. Consider what your opposing counsel's core theory is and how to make your core theory more appealing to the judges than hers. Using your core theory, you should also find ways to rebut your opposing counsel's interpretation of specific cases or facts.

2. Review Specific Arguments

Working from the brief, the advocate should outline and review specific arguments regarding application of the law to the facts in issue. This may require some new thought about which arguments are the most convincing or the most controversial.

a. Ranking the Arguments by Importance

The limited time frame of oral argument means that not all of a party's arguments will be developed fully. Keeping in mind the desired results of the litigation, the advocate should rank arguments in terms of their importance in achieving those results. There is no single method for prioritizing. Some factors to weigh are whether a written argument is simple enough to make orally; what policy considerations may move a judge to rule favorably; what argument the judges are likely to want clarified; what argument is most closely related to the facts; and whether an argument follows or goes against current trends in the law. Arguing for a change in the law may be a strong choice, but often it requires greater policy justification than arguing for the status quo. In addition, you must know exactly what the lower court did and exactly what you seek to have affirmed or reversed.

b. The Merits of the Arguments

Think seriously about the merits of the other party's arguments, despite any flaws you may perceive in their brief. In many cases the court will challenge you by wording the other side's positions better than they do, and you will need to formulate a convincing counter-argument. Be objective about your own arguments, as well. Judges may be skeptical of points that are a "stretch" or that are unsupported by much authority. Sometimes judges may attempt to extract superficial concessions on small points of your argument, in a manner such that each concession appears innocuous until you are shown to have contradicted yourself or abandoned your argument. Review your arguments with attention to points that may be vulnerable so that you can prepare to meet these types of situations.

Sometimes, however, conceding one point that appears weak may save your credibility. For example, if there are several alternative arguments for your side, admitting the weakness of one alternative, if pressed, may enhance your ability to argue for another. Also, if a judge paraphrases your position in a way too unreasonable for you to agree with, you can reword it or concede that this is not a perfect position but it is preferable to the solution suggested by the other side. As long as you know the limits to the principle you are arguing, you will avoid having a judge lead you to admit that extreme applications of your principle will produce absurd results. A good rule of thumb is to be firm on your arguments and also to appear fair.

Often, reading your opponent's brief and playing devil's advocate with your own brief makes it possible to anticipate judges' questions. If a case cited by opposing counsel is truly damaging to your argument, find a way to distinguish it. Review your core theory and think about how it might help explain the case to a doubting judge.

C. STRATEGY AND STYLE

The oral argument should be a conversation with the judges, in which you discuss your view of how the case should be resolved and address any doubts they have about your interpretation of the facts and the law. By providing believable answers that eliminate their doubts, you will persuade them to decide in favor of your client. The judges' questions may not be predictable, but if you are well-prepared and a good listener, you will have no trouble answering any question they may raise.

While oral argument is not a rehearsed play, neither is it an oral reincarnation of the brief. The argument should be lively, vivid, and occasionally improvised. If need be, use a clever illustration to make a point clear. Pick up on the judges' metaphors and hypotheticals, and suggest your own. Often, nothing is more persuasive than using an example that the judges can picture vividly in their minds, because that image is likely to be remembered far beyond your presentation.

Another key preparation strategy is to think about the institutional factors that might influence a judge's attitudes. What arguments are likely to appeal to a particular judge based on ideological preferences? Will the bench be "hot" (confrontational) or "cold," and are the judges likely to have read your brief before your argument? Any predictions as to these factors will be just that — predictions — but often, devoting some thought to these factors will influence the nature of your conversation with the panel.

Similarly, you should know the different advantages of representing the appellant or the appellee. The appellant speaks first and has the opportunity to raise particular issues and to set the tone of the argument. The appellee, on the other hand, can tailor her argument to concerns of the court evinced in questions to the appellant. The opportunity for rebuttal gives appellant the last word, but in another sense, appellee has the upper hand since appellant seeks to overturn a lower court judgment already entered against her.

Both parties should be aware of the standard of review in an appellate argument. Depending on the controlling law, an appellate court may review a case "de novo" (meaning that it can decide the case however it wants, regardless of the district court opinion) or under more limiting standards, such as the "clearly erroneous" or "abuse of discretion" standards, in which the appellate court is limited to considering whether the district court made an obvious mistake. At the very least, you should be ready to advise the court about the applicable standard of review. At best, you can use the standard of review advantageously in making an argument either to respect or to reverse the district court's judgment. (*See* Chapter 1, "Interpreting Facts and Developing Core Theory," Part III, Section E, p.7; Chapter 4, "Writing a Brief," Part II, Section D(3), p.49.)

D. PRACTICE YOUR ARGUMENT

Rehearsal is important for the experience of delivering "live" arguments. Practicing out loud, rather than simply outlining the argument, will help you pay attention to emphasis, timing, pronunciation, and other delivery techniques (*see* this chapter, Part IV, Section B, "Effective Delivery," p.71) and to grow comfortable with the argument's particular vocabulary. It can also lead to substantive improvement of the argument, because flaws in the argument will become more obvious when stated out loud and tested by a practice questioner. Finally, rehearsing builds confidence by making you familiar with the pattern of the argument.

Practicing in simulated court situations is very effective. Practicing alone before audio or videotape recorders may be helpful for some people, although some may be distracted by the technology. Reviewing a recorded performance will expose weaknesses in the argument, awkward phrases, hesitations, wordiness, distracting movements, mumbling, and other flaws in delivery. Even if a video recorder or a practice partner is unavailable, rehearsal of the argument alone out loud is better than nothing. Rehearsal should focus on refining ways of expressing the key concepts, rather than on memorizing a formal speech, which may sound contrived.

II.   Organizing the Oral Argument

A. BASIC STRUCTURE OF ORAL ARGUMENT

This section discusses the various elements contained in a traditional oral presentation. This basic framework is only one of the available options; indeed, the appellee's argument, in particular, may differ from the model as a matter of strategy. However, most oral presentations do conform, at least roughly, to this framework. What would a judge like to know first about the case? What manner of presentation would immediately inform the judge of the central issue? What is an interesting, logical, respectful, and positive approach? The traditional model is one common sense way of answering these questions.

1. The Opening Statement

The opening statement introduces you as counsel and describes the nature of the case. You should introduce yourself in a formal and simple way by giving your name and those of your clients. For example:

> May it please the court, my name is Jane
> Harvey. I represent the appellants, Rebecca and
> Scott Bell-Wesley.

In moot court exercises with teams of speakers, the first speaker should introduce both herself and her teammate. The second speaker will repeat her own name before launching into her half of the argument.

In addition, the first speaker should outline for the court the issues that each of the advocates will develop. A proper introduction of the issues should combine essential facts and legal analysis to describe the case in a nutshell and enable the judges to focus on specific issues presented. The introduction should highlight the core theory and give the court enough information to follow the arguments.

> This case is here on appeal from the Court of Appeals for the State of Ames. The Bell-Wesleys urge this Court to overturn the lower courts' ruling that child-rearing costs are not recoverable in a wrongful pregnancy action.
>
> I will argue that child-rearing damages are recoverable to the same extent as reasonably foreseeable consequences of standard medical malpractice injuries. My co-counsel, Robin Ball, will argue that even if this Court will not award full damages, this Court should adopt the benefit rule and award child-rearing costs offset by the benefit of having the child.

From this statement, the court knows at the outset what the questions are and will listen to the facts with some appreciation of their relevance.

By comparison, an opening that launches into a contorted description of procedural history or immediately begins reciting facts will not give the court adequate background. Confusing openings like these should be avoided:

> This case comes here on appeal to review a judgment of the Superior Court for the State of Ames which, after rejecting Plaintiffs' legal claim, was entered for Defendant.
>
> The facts involve an action by Plaintiffs for full child-rearing costs as damages, resulting from the birth of their son, Frank, after Dr. O'Toole performed a negligent vasectomy on Mr. Bell-Wesley on October 16, 1993.

As these contrasting examples demonstrate, clear presentation is crucial. You should not plunge into facts or procedural history without a true introduction.

2. Concise Outline of Legal Arguments

After introducing yourself and the case, you should give the court a concise outline of the legal arguments you will develop to support your position. The appellant in *Bell-Wesley v. O'Toole,* speaking on the first issue (recovering full damages), might present her outline in the following manner:

> There are two legal bases for the Bell-Wesleys'
> claim for child rearing damages. First, Dr.
> O'Toole's behavior contains all the elements neces-
> sary to prove medical malpractice. Second, awarding
> compensation to the Bell-Wesleys would support
> public policies favoring family planning, self-de-
> termination, and trust between doctor and patient.

This summary outline gives the judges a pattern in which to fit later arguments, indicates the order in which matters will be discussed, and enables the court to defer its questions until the appropriate time. More-over, announcing the arguments at the beginning of a presentation — even if in abbreviated form — will at least communicate that these particular arguments are important, even if lengthy questioning on an early point precludes discussing all of the topics prepared for discussion.

3. Statement of Facts

As in the brief, the oral statement of facts sets the stage for resolving legal issues in a specific factual context. As soon as the court has heard the summary outline of arguments, it will want to know what circum-stances are behind this dispute, since its job is ultimately to favor one party over another.

As your aim is to tell a clear and convincing story, you should not assume that the court already knows the facts. Even when judges are well-prepared, they will not have memorized the case and may not have decided which facts are important. A good statement of facts can therefore set the stage for them to listen to your arguments. On the other hand, time constraints and strategic choices make it advisable to eliminate all but the most relevant facts. You should always keep in mind where your story is going, so that you do not digress on tangents or spend too much time on details.

The statement of facts should be framed and delivered in a manner that presents an identifiable point of view. However, if the facts are too obviously slanted or misleading, you will lose credibility with the court. Therefore, rather than providing an exhaustive chronology, the most important function of the oral statement of facts is drawing attention to key facts that will become important in subsequent arguments. The statement should be as short as possible to achieve the desired goal. In moot court situations, only the first speaker should state the facts, includ-ing facts important to both speakers' arguments.

When representing appellees, you must make a judgment call about how many facts to state. Undisputed facts stated by the appellant usually should not be repeated. However, the appellee can use a statement of facts to tell her own story, dispelling the vision of the case created by the

appellant. Furthermore, if the appellee truly believes that the appellant has omitted or mischaracterized important facts, she can draw attention to these misrepresentations.

4. *The Arguments*

a. Presenting Arguments

You should present your strongest points early in the argument, using an "inverted pyramid" structure: most important/weighty to least. This both attracts the court's attention and ensures that these points are not omitted if time runs out. As in the brief, state conclusions first and then support them with facts and law. The opposite approach (setting out a series of premises that only later lead to conclusions) is often too complicated to be effective because judges will interrupt with questions before you have reached the important part of the argument.

b. Blending Fact and Law

You should organize your presentation with appropriate attention to both fact and law, and make connections between the two as much as possible. An argument that discusses black-letter trends since Blackstone's era without mentioning their relevance to the parties in court, or one that describes the endlessly complex contract negotiations between the parties without alluding once to the legal implications of their dispute, will probably fail. Unless you integrate the factual and legal elements of your argument, no court will ever be able to understand your position or rule in your favor.

The relative proportions of fact and law differ in every case. When asking the court to extend doctrine and create a new rule of law, the attorney should concentrate on legal arguments and explain why the existing rule has led to unfair results in prior cases. On the other hand, if the attorney merely is asking the court to apply an established rule of law, more time should be devoted to explaining the facts and showing how they fit into the established rule.

5. *Conclusion*

Conclude an oral presentation by summarizing the most important arguments. The conclusion should be a brief explanation of the relationship among all of the arguments presented, integrating them into the core theory. Emphasize the strongest arguments in the conclusion. When there is nothing left to say and no further questions, thank the court and end the presentation, even if time is left. A makeshift argument meant to fill the remaining time could weaken the main arguments.

B. APPELLEE'S ARGUMENT

As the traditional appellee's argument is structurally similar to the appellant's, the guidelines listed above will be helpful. Appellee's counsel, just as much as appellant's, should develop an independent core theory, and should not limit herself entirely to a reactive role.

However, the necessity of answering the appellant's argument creates unique issues for appellees. When the two sides explicitly disagree, the appellee may challenge the appellant's assertions directly. This affirmative method brings to the sharp and focused attention of the court the clear distinctions between the two parties' cases. Counsel should listen closely to the appellant's oral presentation and to the questions the judges ask, taking notes as the argument proceeds. Although the appellee's counsel should have a tentative outline prepared before the argument, she should also be ready to respond to issues that obviously concerned the judges when they questioned the other party.

Appellees also enjoy the benefit of arguing to preserve the status quo as embodied in the lower court's decision. Therefore, if the applicable standard of review favors leaving the lower court's decision in place, appellees should emphasize the importance of that standard and appellants' difficulty in meeting it.

C. APPELLANT'S REBUTTAL

At the beginning of the argument, the appellant may wish to reserve time for rebuttal. Rebuttal time should be used to clarify any prior arguments and react to the appellee's presentation. Because it is the court's last impression of the case, rebuttal can be very important.

The time reserved for rebuttal should not be extensive, as reserving too much time may detract from the effectiveness of the main argument. In many circumstances, it may even be effective to decline the use of rebuttal time, indicating to the court that the case as first presented was solid and remains so even after the other side has presented its argument. An ill-prepared or rambling rebuttal can undermine even the best points made in the first argument. Rebuttals can also give the judges an opportunity to ask more difficult questions about the initial argument. Generally, rebuttal time should be used only to contest directly a point made by the appellee.

III.   Questions by the Court

A. THE VALUE OF QUESTIONS

Questions from the court reveal the judges' perceptions of the case, as well as their biases and policy concerns. Listening carefully to the judges' questions and noticing their nonverbal cues make it easier to frame

persuasive answers and budget time. If it is apparent from the nods of the judges or from their questions that they already agree with the position taken on an issue, it may be a good idea to finish discussing that issue relatively soon and move on to a new issue. If the questions indicate that the court disagrees with certain contentions, you should take time to present arguments that might convince the court of the position's validity.

Not every question asked is meant to attack the position presented, so you should not assume that interruption for questions is a hostile act. Some questions are designed to support your view and some are simply points about which the judge is confused and has no preconceived opinion. Furthermore, some "softball" questions are asked to allow the attorney to argue a point more fully. For example, a judge could ask the Bell-Wesleys' counsel:

> What policy goals would be served by allowing
> the Bell-Wesleys to recover child-rearing costs?

You should seize this chance to elucidate your position and impress a judge who is already an "ally." Don't miss the opportunity presented by a judge who offers you an open question, restates your argument in a new way or supports your position with a new argument.

B. EFFECTIVE ANSWERING

1. Be Responsive

To respond to questions adequately, you must understand what the judge has asked. If the question's wording is unclear, ask the judge to repeat or rephrase it. If the substantive implications of a question are unclear, repeat what the judge appears to be asking and inquire whether that is what the judge means. It is often wise to pause and reflect briefly on the question before beginning to speak. Taking a few seconds to collect your thoughts usually results in a more focused response. A prompt but disorganized answer may confuse the judge further, leading either to more questions or to a weak showing on the issue.

A judge's questions may spring from confusion; misunderstanding; concern about the consequences of broadening a legal rule; hostility born of a personal conviction that a position is wrong; or a genuine desire to help the speaker regain footing after tough interrogation from a less than friendly colleague. Answers should be framed to address the judge's concerns, as evasive answers usually provoke judges to repeat questions and badger the speakers. In some cases, if a judge finds a party to be unduly evasive, she may grow exasperated and simply rule against that party. A judge also likes to think that her question is unique and will probably resent what sounds like a "pat" answer.

If the judge tries to elicit a "yes" or "no" response that seems to corner the speaker into a contrived position, the speaker should provide the one-word response but follow up quickly by explaining why the question is not so clear-cut; unwillingness to answer at all signals disrespect.

2. Advocate

You should use questions to advance the argument, even if the questions require bringing up a point before its planned place. Questions can also be used to put a positive spin on the client's position. You could make a concession, but show that it is not inconsistent with your client's case or is minor in comparison with the main point. You could also show that the judge's concern is even more reason to find for your client. Once the court seems satisfied with an answer, make a smooth transition from that response to another related topic. Maintaining continuity and minimizing awkward silences is important, although a brief pause between arguments can be used advantageously.

Using a question as a vehicle to advance a line of argument is not an easy skill to master. The following is an example of how an attorney for the appellant in *Bell-Wesley v. O'Toole* might proceed.

When a judge asks:

> If the Bell-Wesleys didn't want to pay child-rearing costs, why did they conceive children on three prior occasions?,

the appellants' attorney might answer:

> Your Honor, it may seem logical that if the Bell-Wesleys were prepared to assume the financial burden of raising children in the past, there is no reason they should not be similarly situated now. Before experiencing the tremendous emotional anguish accompanying the births and deaths of three deformed children, the Bell-Wesleys had indeed decided to take on the financial burden of raising children. However, after suffering immeasurably when each of their children died in infancy, they made a conscious choice to forego having children. Once they made that decision, they no longer accounted for children in their financial decisions and long-term planning. The issue is not whether, since they previously conceived and gave birth to children, they should now be presumed to be in the same financial position to raise Frank Michael. Rather, the issue is whether Dr. O'Toole's negligence caused the Bell-Wesleys a financial loss. Dr. O'Toole gave the Bell-Wesleys reason to believe that they would not have children and to plan their life accordingly. Thus, he must be held liable for all the foreseeable consequences of his negligence, including the costs of raising a healthy child to majority.

The first sentence of this sample answer restates the question. By restating the question counsel has shown that she fully understands the question asked. (Indeed, the judge could have interrupted and corrected any misperception of the question.) Then, counsel uses the question as a platform to advance her argument that damages ought to be awarded; to remind the judge of the Bell-Wesleys' personal suffering; and to reframe the question from "Why did the parents attempt to have children before?" to "What responsibility does Dr. O'Toole have for his negligence now?"

Good preparation is the key to answering questions. Although it is natural to feel unprepared and apprehensive going into oral argument, an advocate who has reviewed the record, authorities, and briefs will often be pleasantly surprised and find that the court's questions are manageable. Finally, if there seems to be no good answer to a question, be very honest with the court. Being evasive is more detrimental than simply saying, "I don't know."

C. PARTICULAR TYPES OF QUESTIONS JUDGES MIGHT ASK

1. *Questions Seeking Information About the Facts*

If the statement of facts is adequate and gives the court some idea of which facts are crucial, many time-consuming questions may be avoided. If factual items are central, a judge will often want to read them directly from the record. Judges are also likely to ask about material facts missing from the record.

Questions about the facts may also come from the judge who feels that you have wandered too far from the case into an abstract discourse on the law. This can be avoided by wording arguments to bring out the facts of the case. For instance, in making an argument concerning plaintiffs' reliance on a statement by the defendant, counsel might say, "Mr. and Mrs. Bell-Wesley relied on Dr. O'Toole's assurance that Scott Bell-Wesley's vasectomy had been successful," rather than dryly saying, "Reliance by the plaintiffs is indicated in this case."

2. *Questions About "Policy Considerations"*

Questions of this nature are often phrased as follows:

> Counsel, is it possible that allowing recovery of child-rearing costs from the doctor will create an atmosphere in which doctors are deterred from performing vasectomies generally?

Here the court wants to hear a fuller exposition of the relevant factors to a decision, and possibly a response to opposing policy considerations.

Sometimes, questions of this sort are phrased more argumentatively:

```
    But, counsel, isn't it settled that the benefits
of the birth outweigh the burdens?
```

The form of the question does not mean that the judge has necessarily decided against the position advanced. It may well be that her thinking is currently adverse to that position. The advocate should not give up, but rather should try to put the point in a new light and to change the judge's mind.

3. Questions Directed at the Authorities Cited

When a judge asks about a cited case, she wants something more than a dry recitation of the facts and the holding. She wants to know how it relates to the case being argued. Is it binding in this jurisdiction? Does it show an existing framework of law into which the desired result must fit? Can a valid and consistent exception to the precedent be made without detracting from the force of the precedent as a whole?

The judge also wants to know why the earlier court decided as it did. What considerations controlled the decision? Has the weight to be given these factors changed since the court decided the earlier case?

In a case of first impression, the judge will need to know why the precedent you cite is persuasive, or why the precedent your opponent cites is unpersuasive, in formulating a new doctrine. Is the precedent grounded in sound public policy? Will it be relevant to future situations? Will it give rise to an efficient system of justice?

4. Questions Directed at Particular Legal Arguments

Questions of this type test an argument's logic. Loose statements of holdings, overbroad analogies, and imprecise wording can unleash a veritable barrage of questions.

Some questions test knowledge of the case and depth of understanding of the surrounding law. Judges often want to know how far an argument will take the court down an uncharted path. In order to prevent the application of a certain doctrine, be prepared to deliver what is often called a "parade of horribles," the negative implications of accepting opposing counsel's line of argument. Think through the implications of doctrines advocated by your opponent in order to be ready to offer responsive answers that might help the court decide the case.

Judges may ask hypothetical questions to get at the future implications of your argument. They may ask small hypotheticals step-by-step, using leading questions, until the original argument appears to be founded on faulty reasoning. Answering hypotheticals, then, requires vigilance and attention to the direction the judge is going with the questions.

Keep in mind that the case being argued involves specific parties in a single fact situation. Weaving the facts neatly into your answers can prevent the advocate from getting trapped into defending a broad general principle against all possible attacks.

D. QUESTIONING IN TEAM SITUATIONS

Although judges should refrain from questioning one member of the team about issues for which the other member is primarily responsible, each co-counsel should understand her partner's basic arguments. If questioning becomes too specific, ask the court either to permit co-counsel to return to the lectern or, in the case of the first oralist, to await your teammate's later appearance. If properly prepared, the second speaker may also take the opportunity to cover crucial points that her co-counsel inadvertently omitted and to develop further any answers that may have been inadequate.

IV.   Presenting the Oral Argument

A. BE YOURSELF

If there is one general rule of presenting an argument, it is "Be yourself." An ordinarily even-tempered and moderate person usually should not affect a flashy, fist-pounding display of rhetoric, because trying too hard to create a different, "effective" personality for the argument may divert energy from the issues in the case, and may be hard to maintain. There is no single right way to argue a case, and the more comfortable you are, the more effective the argument is likely to be. You should assess your personality and speaking style ahead of time and think of ways to use your unique strengths in the argument and to polish your own delivery.

B. EFFECTIVE DELIVERY

A clear presentation that is easy to follow is crucial no matter what the speaker's personal style. The speaker should not read from notes unless absolutely necessary, because a paper barrier between court and counsel inhibits effective presentation. The best advocates have a thorough knowledge of relevant materials. This does not mean memorizing case citations. Rather, it means dealing quickly and surely with the issues, calling forth relevant arguments without fumbling through a mound of written materials for a case or fact. Eye contact with the judges is extremely helpful, both in terms of keeping the judges focused on you and convincing them that the argument is defensible. With good eye contact, you are most likely to involve the judges in an active process.

Quoting cases to support arguments is sometimes useful, but quotes should be short and used sparingly if at all. In general, paraphrasing the language of cases cited in the brief is a more effective way of communicating their essence to the judges and a more efficient use of time.

71

The most effective oral arguments have the tone of a conversation rather than a speech. In this way, oral argument is much different than presentation to a jury. It need not be quite as heightened or dramatized as a statement before a jury, partially because the judges know the applicable law thoroughly, and partially because judges (unlike juries) may interrupt you. Still, within this conversation, you should remember that your goal is to persuade and to get across a point of view. Toward that end, you should speak clearly and convey your belief in what you are arguing.

You should avoid legalese and other jargon as long as there is a simpler way to make your point. Overly complex sentence structure may make your argument hard to follow. The attention span in listening to a speaker is significantly less than when reading a brief. Therefore, it is useful preparation to take an especially complicated sentence from the brief and figure out how to express it orally by colloquializing it, simplifying it, and imbuing it with feeling without becoming too informal.

To some extent the conversational character of a presentation will depend on whether the court asks numerous questions. But even if the judges remain quiet, the lawyer should not appear to lecture or speak down to the court. Some general points of public speaking to keep in mind are:

- **Be heard**. Speak a little more slowly than in everyday conversation. Project your voice, as you will be at some distance from the judges rather than across a desk from them. You can practice projecting by aiming your voice at the back of the room. People who are soft-spoken may have to adjust to the feeling of projecting. Projecting, however, does not mean yelling. Also, be careful not to mumble or to swallow the ends of sentences.

- **Use proper emphasis**. Without emphasis on key words, you may risk falling into a sing-song pattern where your voice goes up and down arbitrarily, losing the judges' attention. Stressing certain words, or even certain complete concepts, and moving relatively quickly through others will show the listener what your priorities are. Good verbal phrasing will lead the listener toward points that reinforce your core theory.

- **Use the pause**. This device, when used sparingly and judiciously, serves to stress the points being made and helps to regain a judge's attention when she has become preoccupied with a cited passage in the record or brief.

- **Be aware of body language**. You should maintain eye contact with the judges and appear physically calm and collected. Standing straight and avoiding fidgeting will make you more effective because any gesture that you use for emphasis will have the desired effect. For instance, waving hands, pounding

the podium too fiercely or playing nervously with hands can be distracting. Pointing at the judges can be disrespectful. On the other hand, small and expressive hand gestures (such as showing the "broad" scope of an argument, weighing alternatives, or extending a hand to the judges inviting them to agree) can be effective. On the whole, it is easier to listen to someone who appears composed and does not distract attention with nervous movements.

It is unrealistic to expect to be allowed to deliver a complete prepared speech. In fact, the procedural rules for the federal appellate courts prohibit the reading of briefs at argument. Some speakers feel most comfortable after writing out at least the first minute (about a page) of their argument. Although reading this introduction may make the opening moments easier, counsel usually should resist the temptation to read. Use notes as a back-up, but focus on talking to the judges and maintaining eye contact.

C. HAVE A "VOICE"

The "voice" of an oral argument is the stylistic manifestation of a core theory. The speaker should have an identifiable point of view, an emotional perspective on the case, both in approaching the legal arguments and in presenting the client's story. This point of view is essentially the core theory translated into the speaker's choices of words, emphases, and tone of voice. One step toward articulating a voice is finding a value you can represent — equity, accountability for wrongs, compassion, discipline, remedying past imbalances of power — and making yourself sound like the embodiment of that value. Another is approaching the court in a way that fits best with the client's position. For instance, you could frame your argument as a plea to be merciful and fair; as a request to make an exception to a rule; as a call to protect constitutional rights; as a rallying cry to reform the law; as a warning that unless the judge takes your position, negative consequences will result; as an admonition to recognize the limits of the court's power; or as an invocation of the force of tradition.

The voice of an advocate for the Bell-Wesleys may emphasize equity, as illustrated by the unfairness of leaving unremedied the doctor's breach of patients' fundamental rights. Alternatively, she may invoke compassion for the Bell-Wesleys who had three deformed children and wanted to ensure that they would not have more. Dr. O'Toole's lawyer may choose to adopt a voice of respect for life, describing the folly of asking the legal system to recognize a "wrong" in the birth of a healthy baby, and the warped values that characterize that baby solely as a financial burden. He may alternatively choose to emphasize the limits of doctors' liability, and embody the voice of caution: if we allow such high damages to be assessed against doctors, then they will be deterred from doing socially valuable work.

An important corollary to developing a voice is preserving credibility. Credibility can be undermined by misleading the judges about the facts of the case; making personal attacks on the other speakers; sounding unconvinced of your own argument; being unable to support a point when asked about it; sounding apocalyptic or hyperbolic; or refusing to concede even minor points at any cost. The point of a voice, or core theory, is to develop a believable approach to the case.

D. ATTITUDE TOWARD THE COURT

Your attitude toward the court should be one of respectful equality — not servile to the court, but according judges due deference. Even in the heat of hard questioning, you should be receptive and cooperative, and should not show annoyance at the trend of the questioning. Giving definite answers to the court's questions, speaking with an animated and positive tone, and being confident of the strength of the argument is more likely to promote listening than adopting an aggressive interpersonal manner. Hostile behavior can be perceived as "defensive" and may suggest that you are unable to support your own argument.

You should attempt to be helpful to the court and to make sure everything is clear. You should not treat anything as obvious or as a waste of time, but rather should act as a true "counselor" and respond empathetically to judges' concerns. Of course, if questions appear to be repetitive or distracting, you can indicate calmly but firmly that you will now move on to the next point.

E. WHAT TO TAKE TO COURT

Given the limited amount of time allotted for oral argument and the need for continuous presentation and dialogue, the opportunity to refer to materials is limited. However, it is still important to have the record and briefs accessible at the lectern. The court may ask questions that specifically refer to these documents. Tabbing or clipping pertinent pages in the record and briefs will make use of these documents easier. Two other kinds of materials may be helpful. First, a short outline of points to be covered will keep you organized without encouraging reading verbatim. Second, note cards containing important facts and quotations from cases may be useful.

F. HANDLING MISCITATIONS AND MISREPRESENTATIONS BY OPPOSING COUNSEL

Bring any miscitations and misrepresentations of opposing counsel to the court's attention when they are important to the case. If a misrepresentation influences an essential argument; if the court will be unable to find the correct citation; or if the judges' questions reveal that they do not realize that a fact or doctrine has been misrepresented, you should call attention to the misrepresentation. When appropriate, corrections can

help your credibility. However, you should not appear to be attacking opposing counsel personally. For instance, an advocate in the Bell-Wesley case might say:

> With all due respect to Ms. Harvey, it appears that Appellant claims that Dr. O'Toole guaranteed the 100% effectiveness of the vasectomy. If the Court would please refer to Exhibit 4 in the record, the Court will see that the Bell-Wesleys signed an acknowledgment that Dr. O'Toole had informed them of the chance that any given vasectomy would not be successful.

G. FORMAL CONDUCT

A few customs of formal conduct should be observed in oral argument. The customs do not vary much from courtroom to courtroom. When beginning the argument, speakers should rise and say, "May it please the court," or "If the court pleases," before introducing themselves. In answering questions, address the judge as "Your Honor." In referring to members of the court, "Judge Smith" or "The Chief Justice" is appropriate. Opposing counsel should be referred to as such, or as "Ms. Overton" or "counsel for the defendant" but never as "my opponent." Associate counsel is called "my colleague," "my associate," "co-counsel," or "Ms. Jones."

APPENDIX A

General Rules of Style and Citation of Authorities

Attorneys often remark that in legal practice form is half the battle. This Appendix is designed to facilitate learning of correct citation form and general rules of style. While individual states, localities, and organizations may require unique forms, the materials presented here follow those dictated by *The Bluebook: A Uniform System of Citation* (16th ed. 1996), published by the Harvard Law Review Association. As you will quickly discover, *The Bluebook* is the most widely used reference for citation form in the United States, serving as a reliable default system of rules in the absence of specific direction. However, be forewarned that particular courts and jurisdictions may deviate substantially from *The Bluebook*. Also, many law firms simplify the rules of citation and style for internal use. It is important to remember that *The Bluebook* primarily focuses on the forms to be used by legal scholars and academics. Most of the rules are intended for works that will be published in law journals or other secondary sources. Thus, the rules are extraordinarily detailed and exhaustive. However, the bottom line is that *The Bluebook* sets the standard for the profession; citations written in accordance with *The Bluebook* are sure to be complete and informative. *The Bluebook* should be a constant companion of the student learning the intricacies of legal citation for the first time. The best way to become familiar with the rules is to use them.

Recognizing that *The Bluebook* can be overwhelming, this Appendix highlights the relevant rules for the practitioner. The rules in this Appendix are current as of September 1996. For areas outside the scope of this Appendix, or to update the information presented here, the reader should consult *The Bluebook* directly. Any conflicts between the two sources should be resolved in favor of *The Bluebook*.

Part I of this Appendix addresses the general rules governing the writing of legal documents. Part II presents the elements of a legal citation. Part III deals with the purpose and weight of citations and the treatment of multiple authorities cited for the same point. The actual form of citations is dealt with in Part IV (cases) and Part V (statutes and constitutions). Citations in this chapter do not refer to actual cases.

I. General Rules of Style

A. ABBREVIATIONS

Citations to authority in practitioners' documents are placed directly in the body of the document rather than in footnotes. They appear in citation sentences or clauses, as well as in textual sentences. The distinction between these two uses is spelled out in practitioners' note P.2 and rule 10.2 of *The Bluebook*. Basically, when referring to a case directly in a textual sentence or in the Table of Citations, follow the forms delineated in rule 10.2.1. When citing to cases in a separate citation sentence, use rule 10.2.2. The following examples illustrate the difference between the use of a case in a textual sentence and the use of a case in a citation sentence:

Textual sentence

Unlike the baby born to the plaintiffs in Medical Federation, Inc. v. Scott, 22 F.3d 199 (10th Cir. 1995), the Bell-Wesleys have a healthy son. In Medical Federation, the court held that parents of a congenitally deformed child could recover the costs of raising the child to majority. Id. at 203.

Citation sentence

The Bell-Wesleys cannot recover the costs of raising a healthy son. Cf. Medical Fed'n, Inc. v. Scott, 22 F.3d 199 (10th Cir. 1995) (awarding plaintiffs damages for the costs of raising a congenitally deformed child).

Cases which serve as the focal point of analysis may be presented as part of the text of the document. Cases which merely support or serve as a point of comparison to a given proposition, but which do not merit more extensive treatment, will commonly be referenced in a citation sentence. Generally, in a textual sentence, words are spelled out in their entirety, whereas in a citation sentence, the words are abbreviated according to rule 10.2 and table T.6 of *The Bluebook*.

Well-known statutes and agencies may be designated by initials after the full name has been written out once. The periods are omitted.

"The National Labor Relations Board has done commendable work. At its inception, the NLRB was not . . . ."

"United States" is never abbreviated in a case name. In a textual sentence, it may be abbreviated when used as an adjective. *See The Bluebook*, rule 6.1. Names of states are abbreviated only in citations.

B. CAPITALIZATION

The following words are capitalized only in the indicated situations:

"Act" — when referring to a specific act: the National Labor Relations Act . . . the Act.

"Circuit" — when used with the circuit number: First Circuit.

"Code" — when referring to a specific code: the 1939 and 1954 Codes.

"Constitution" — when referring to the United States Constitution or to any constitution in full: Constitution of the State of California. **Exception:** federal constitution. References to amendments to the Constitution, the "Bill of Rights," and other parts of the U.S. Constitution are capitalized in textual sentences, but not in citations: First Amendment; U.S. Const. amend. I.

"Court" — when naming any court in full; otherwise, only when referring to the United States Supreme Court or when referring to the court receiving the document: the Supreme Court of Illinois; the [state] supreme court; the court of appeals; the Court of Appeals for the Fifth Circuit; this Court.

"Federal" — only when the word it modifies is capitalized: Federal Aviation Administration; federal law.

"Justice" or "Judge" — when referring to a Justice of the United States Supreme Court or when giving the name of a specific justice or judge: Justice Ginsburg; Justice Handler of the New Jersey Supreme Court; Judge Llewenstein.

"Rule" — when part of a proper name given in full: Federal Rules of Evidence; Federal Rules of Civil Procedure.

"State" — when the word it modifies is capitalized; when referring to a state as a party to litigation or as a governmental actor; and if it is part of the full title of a state: California State University at Fresno; the State filed early; the State of Washington.

"Statute" — when part of a proper name given in full: Statute of Anne.

"Plaintiff," "Defendant," "Appellant," "Appellee" — only when referring to parties to the action which is the subject of the court document or memorandum: `The plaintiffs' bar benefits from class action rules.  In this case, Plaintiff seeks attorney's fees in the amount of $1.5 billion.`

Titles of court documents — when the documents have been filed in the action at bar. Do not capitalize generic references to court documents: `Plaintiff's Memorandum of Points and Authorities in Opposition to Motion for Summary Judgment exceeds the page limits established by this Court.  Defendant's motion conforms to the Court's requirements and will be granted.`

C. ITALICIZATION AND UNDERLINING

Although italicization and underlining are technically interchangeable, practitioners generally default to underlining. Italicization or underlining is proper in the following circumstances:

1. Case Names. The names of both parties and the "v." between the names should be underlined. Short forms must also be underlined: "The Jones case held . . . ." The Latin words in a case name are also underlined: In re McLaughlin; Ex parte Savin.

2. Introductory Signals. All introductory signals are underlined: see also; see generally; cf.; but see.

3. Foreign Words and Phrases. Underlining of foreign words and phrases is determined by the extent of the word's incorporation into common English usage. Words which have been fully assimilated should not be underlined. There is a presumption that Latin words frequently used in legal writing constitute "common English." Consult a current dictionary for aid in making this determination.

    a. **Foreign Words Always Underlined:** ex parte, ex rel., in re, inter alia, inter se, passim, quaere, semble, sic., sub nom., infra, and supra.

    b. **Foreign Words Not Underlined:** ad hoc, a fortiori, amicus curiae, bona fide, certiorari, de novo, dictum, ipso facto, mandamus, per curiam, per se, prima facie, pro rata, quid pro quo, quo warranto, res judicata, stare decisis, and subpoena (and its modifiers).

Additionally, *The Bluebook,* practitioners' note P.1, lists other categories of words that are underlined, such as names of publications.

D. NUMERALS, SYMBOLS, AND DATES

1. Numerals. Numbers under 100 should always be written out in the body of a document, except when relating to a statistical study, a dollar amount, or when used in a date:

> The dean had been sleeping for eighty-seven days.

> Only 22% of those surveyed prefer New York to San Francisco.

> She has been in jail since June 4, 1972.

Numbers should also be spelled out if they begin a sentence. There are special rules for numbers that contain decimal points, round numbers, and numbers appearing in a series. Refer to *The Bluebook*, rule 6.2, for further guidance.

2. Symbols. The word "section" must be spelled out, unless part of a citation or the first word of a sentence:

> 18 U.S.C. § 1945

> That section allows recovery of attorney's fees for successful plaintiffs in citizen suits.

The dollar sign ($) and percent symbol (%) should only appear with numerals, but a symbol should never begin a sentence. If numerals are not used in a sentence, the words "dollar" and "percent" must be spelled out.

3. Dates. The month of a date should always be written out:

> She was born on March 14.

E. QUOTATIONS

Quotations under fifty words in length, set off by quotation marks, are regularly incorporated in the text. Those more than fifty words in length must be indented and single spaced. Indented quotations are not set off by quotation marks. Attribution of an indented quotation should not be indented. For detailed treatment of indented quotations, refer to rule 5 of *The Bluebook*.

1. Placement of Quotation Marks. Periods and commas should always be placed inside quotation marks. All other punctuation marks should be placed outside the quotation marks unless they are part of the material quoted.

2.   Omissions from Quotations. Omission of material from a quotation must be indicated in certain circumstances. All omissions of material from sentences must be indicated, as well as omissions of sentences and paragraphs from quotations. Sentences and paragraphs are not "omitted" unless they originally fell *within* the quoted material. *See The Bluebook*, rule 5.3.

a. Short Quotations. Phrases may be quoted without indicating omissions before or after the quotation, unless it would be misleading not to indicate the omission.

```
In all such circumstances, the courts
"balance the benefits with the costs."
```

b. Clarification of Noun, Pronoun, or Verb. When a bracket insertion clarifies a noun or pronoun or changes the tense or number of a verb, the corresponding omission need not be indicated. Brackets may also be used to change the number of a noun.

```
"The employee[s] did not know [they were]
being watched."
```

c. Omission at the Beginning of a Sentence. The omission of language at the beginning of a quoted sentence is indicated by capitalizing and placing in brackets the first letter of the first word of the quoted section. An ellipsis is improper (three spaced periods set off by a space before the first period and after the last period).

```
"[S]he is capable of moving mountains."
```

d. Omission in the Middle of a Sentence. Omitting language from the middle of a sentence is indicated by inserting an ellipsis.

```
"The tunes were sung without harmony . . .
resulting in a miserable school musical."
```

e. Omission at the End of a Sentence. Omitting language at the end of a sentence is indicated by inserting an ellipsis and end punctuation.

```
"Whenever we travel, we are reminded that
life is an adventure . . .!"
```

f. Omission from the Middle of a Multi-Sentence Quotation. The omission of language in the middle of a quotation after the end of a sentence that is followed by the rest of the quotation

is indicated by retaining the period at the end of the quoted sentence and inserting an ellipsis. There should be no space before the period ending the first quoted sentence.

> "Two birds flew over the cuckoo's nest. . . .
> Twelve days later, I understood the
> significance of the birds."

3. Alterations in Quotations

a. Added Underlining or Omitted Footnotes. Alterations of the quotation, such as the addition of underlining or the omission of footnotes or citations in the quoted material, are indicated by parentheticals at the end of the quotation's citation.

> Griswold v. Oregon, 65 U.S. 150, 161 (1995)
> (emphasis added); People v. McManus, 13 F.
> Supp. 57, 60 (D. Or. 1996) (citations
> omitted).

b. Change of Letter. Changing a lower case letter to a capital letter or vice versa is indicated by bracketing the altered letter.

> "[T]en others agreed with her."

c. Supplementary or Explanatory Words. Supplementary or explanatory words inserted in a quotation must be enclosed in brackets. Language enclosed by parentheses in the original should also be enclosed by regular parentheses in the quotation.

> "War and Peace is the acknowledged
> masterpiece (in any language) [not including
> Swahili]."

4. Page Numbers of Quoted Materials.
Indicate the page upon which a quotation begins and, if it continues to another page, the page on which it ends.

> Colorado v. Recklie, 330 P.2d 1284, 1286-87
> (Colo. 1996).

F. TECHNICAL WORDS OF REFERENCE

1. "Id." Use "*Id.*" to cite to immediately preceding cases, statutes, or constitutions appearing in the same general discussion. Do not use "*supra*," which is used in law journal footnotes and as discussed below. A good rule of thumb is that citations indicated by "*id.*" should not be more than a couple of paragraphs apart and certainly should not span discussion sections. Use "*id.*" only if it allows the reader readily to identify the cited authority. When in doubt, provide a short form or full citation.

2. "Supra." *"Supra"* is appropriate for sources other than cases, statutes, or constitutions. It may be used when the complete citation of the material appeared previously in the same general discussion:

> See Restatement of Torts, supra.

When citing to a particular page of a source previously cited in full, use the following form:

> Restatement of Torts, supra, at 35.

Refer to *The Bluebook*, practitioners' note P.4(d) and rule 4.2 for further details.

3. References to the Record. References to the record should follow the cited material with the letter "R" separated from the page number(s) by a period and enclosed in parentheses:

> (R.17)
>
> (R.14-16)
>
> (R.20,23)

A citation to the record is not underlined. References to the record are often governed by local rule. *The Bluebook* shows how to cite to particular documents which make up the record of a given case. *See The Bluebook*, practitioners' note P.7. For purposes of an introductory legal writing class, the more simplistic (R.10) will suffice.

4. References to Footnotes. References to footnotes in a work are made using the letter "n." or "nn." for multiple footnotes:

> S. Williston, Sales 63, 64 n.7, 65 nn.9-11 (rev. ed. 1948).

5. References to Briefs. References to the briefs in a case should appear as follows:

> Def.'s Br. Supp. Summ. J. at 20.
>
> Pl.'s Br. Opp'n. Summ. J. at 7.

G. TABLE OF CITATIONS

1. Citation of Cases. The rules of style for citation of cases in textual sentences also apply in the Table of Citations. The cases are listed in alphabetical order. Cases, statutes, and secondary materials should be presented separately. (See the Tables of Citations in the sample briefs in *Bell-Wesley v. O'Toole*, pp.159, 176.)

2. *Citation of Statutes.* For a good summary guide to statute citation, refer to the short forms table in *The Bluebook*, rule 12.9.

a. **Abbreviations.** The first reference to a statute should always be complete and detailed.

```
Me. Rev. Stat. Ann. tit. 2, § 1 (West 1980).
```

However, subsequent references are governed by rule 12.9 of *The Bluebook*, which permits extensive abbreviation.

In text

```
section 1
```

In citation sentence

```
§ 1
```

Where only one statute is discussed throughout a legal document, it may be referred to simply as "the Act," or "section 1."

b. **Location in the Table of Citations.** Statutes are primary authorities and should be listed immediately following cases in the Table of Citations.

3. *Citation of Secondary Authorities.* All secondary authorities, such as books and periodicals, are grouped under the heading "Miscellaneous" in the Table of Citations. They should appear in alphabetical order. The rules for citation of secondary authorities are detailed and lengthy. Refer to *The Bluebook* for specific citation forms.

H. A NOTE ON SPACING WITHIN CITATIONS

There are many different rules concerning the spacing of citations in legal materials. This Appendix follows the rules outlined in *The Bluebook*. The practitioner should refer to the specific rules governing citation to the authorities of different jurisdictions and sources presented in tables T.1–T.5 of *The Bluebook*. Note that single capitals are "closed up" unless the resulting citation would be confusing, while most other letters and numbers are separated by a space.

```
28 F.3d 199 (10th Cir. 1988).
19 P.2d 222 (Cal. 1991).
48 So. 3d 1882 (Miss. 1992).
12 F. Supp. 999 (D.D.C. 1991).
98 N.E.2d 1236 (N.Y. 1988).
```

II.   Necessary Elements of a Citation

Citations must convey certain essential information. Each citation should (1) identify the authority; (2) indicate where it can be found (for cases, this includes the reporter and the relevant jurisdiction); (3) credit the "author" of the authority; (4) provide the date of the authority; and (5) suggest the purpose for which the authority is cited, as well as its weight.

A. IDENTIFICATION OF AUTHORITY

The case name must be stated. Where several different cases are decided with one opinion, or the case name is unusually long, the case name should be abbreviated. When referring to a case using a short form, you will mostly use the name which appears first in the case report. Thus, if the case were <u>Jonesie Skiing, Inc. v. Porgie</u>, the short form would reference only <u>Jonesie Skiing</u>. However, where the first named party is identified by a common name, use the second named party in subsequent references. Thus, the short form of <u>Brown v. Porgie</u> should reference <u>Porgie</u>, rather than <u>Brown</u>. The goal is ease of identification.

B. WHERE THE AUTHORITY MAY BE FOUND

The "location" of the authority is the publication in which it has been printed. When the authority is a judicial decision, it is customary to refer to both the official and the unofficial reporters, if they are available, when submitting the document to courts of the state issuing the decision. However, in all other documents, omit the official reporter citation. United States Supreme Court cases are cited only to the United States Reports, if therein. Refer to *The Bluebook*, table T.1, for rules by jurisdiction, keeping in mind that table T.1 does not account for local practice rules. In any event, both volume and page numbers are necessary in all case citations.

If the authority is an article, the volume of the periodical in which it appears and the number of the page on which it begins are necessary. A treatise citation should contain the volume and section in which it can be found. Other books are cited similarly except that the author's name and page numbers are used. Refer to *The Bluebook*, rules 15 and 16.

C. INDICATION OF "AUTHOR"

Counsel must indicate the person or persons who wrote or stand behind the printed words on which she relies. If the authority is a case, the citation must precisely identify the court which decided the case. For state cases, this will usually be accomplished by reference to the official report in which the opinion appears, since most official reports cover only

the highest court of the state. For instance, <u>Snow v. Wragg</u>, 303 Mass. 264 (1900), shows that the Supreme Judicial Court of Massachusetts decided the case, for it is the only court reported in the Massachusetts Reports. However, some official reports cover more than the highest court. Almost all unofficial reporters cover more than one court. If the case is in one of these latter classes of reporters, the court must be indicated parenthetically:

> <u>Muir v. Alsup</u>, 221 Misc. 498, 50 N.Y.S.2d 897 (N.Y. Sup. Ct. 1944).

If the identity of the court is obvious from the name of the reporter, the court of decision need not be indicated even if it is not the highest court in the jurisdiction:

> <u>Van Allen v. Semmi</u>, 24 Ariz. App. 316, 217 P.2d 408 (1965).

For federal cases, a date and court parenthetical following the citation must include the district or circuit from which the case came.

> <u>Muggins v. Alabama</u>, 12 F. Supp. 486 (D. Ala. 1993).

> <u>Notoch v. Louisiana</u>, 13 F.2d 1227 (1st Cir. 1990).

Similarly, citation to state cases appearing in regional reporters must indicate the particular state court which rendered the decision.

> <u>Ranger v. Markus</u>, 19 P.3d 990 (Wa. 1994).

> <u>Sophie v. Ellie</u>, 122 N.E.2d 1555 (Ill. Ct. App. 1994).

Correct state court citation forms, such as indications of a decision printed in a regional reporter, but emanating from a state appellate court, can be found in table T.1 of *The Bluebook*.

D. DATE

The year in which the case was decided, the article written, the statute enacted or amended, or the treatise published must be given parenthetically. The date may have direct bearing on the weight which the court will attach to the authority since social conditions or policy may well have changed since the time of the decision, or the authority may be so old and oft-cited as to be considered a bulwark of the jurisdiction's jurisprudence. Similarly, extremely current cases binding on the court will be of high precedential value, as they represent the latest resolution of the contentious issue.

III.   Indication of Purpose and Weight; Order for Multiple Authorities

Proper citation of all authorities (cases, treatises, statutes, etc.) involves indicating the purpose of the citation and the weight (importance) that should be attached to it. This is accomplished through the use of introductory signals and parentheticals.

Citations are often grouped in "sentences." A new citation sentence is introduced with an introductory signal. Within a sentence, citations are separated by semicolons. All authorities supporting a proposition should be introduced before authorities opposing the proposition. The authorities and signals are listed in the order presented below.

The absence of a signal before a citation indicates that the authority cited is the source of a direct quotation or identifies an authority referred to in the text. Although *The Bluebook* does not suggest parenthetical information following citations for which no signal is required, in nearly all instances, parenthetical information should be provided. If counsel treats the authority extensively, a parenthetical after the first reference to the authority may be unnecessary. However, if the authority is not further used, a parenthetical should be provided.

A. SIGNALS INDICATING PURPOSE

1. Authorities Supporting the Proposition. When authorities support the proposition advanced, various degrees of support are indicated by the absence of any express signal and by the use of *"e.g.," "accord," "see," "see also,"* and *"cf."*

a. [No Signal]. Use [no signal] when the case identifies the source of a quotation or an authority referred to in the text.

> The court noted that "thirty other states have already considered the wrongful birth issue." Schumaker v. Phleger, 42 P.2d 1391, 1393 (Haw. 1994).

b. *"Accord."* *"Accord"* should be used when two or more authorities clearly support a proposition, but the text quotes only one. It always follows [no signal]. Similarly, the law of one jurisdiction may be cited as in accord with that of another jurisdiction if the law is exactly the same.

> Accord Maguire v. McCurdy, 325 U.S. 6 (1945).

Or, after the principal case:

> Bordwin v. Ames, 98 U.S. 64 (1878); accord Chase v. Freeman, 300 U.S. 27 (1937).

c. *"See."* *"See"* indicates that the asserted opinion or conclusion is stated or supported by the cited authority.

> The courts should take a liberal view toward the benefit rule in the wrongful pregnancy context. See Gordon v. Cushing, 251 F.2d 8, 12 (3d Cir. 1955) (noting that the benefit rule is particularly appropriate where grave matters of social policy are concerned).

d. *"See also."* Use *"see also"* to cite additional cases that directly support a point which counsel has already supported with analysis from another case. Follow the citation with a parenthetical explaining the material's relevance.

> See also Roberts v. Stern, 234 F. 12 (D.C. Cir. 1938) (stating that the standard of review in Fourth Amendment cases is clear error); LeClair v. Presser, 84 Or. 714, 402 P.2d 102 (1965) (same).

e. *"Cf."* If the cited case or other source material expresses a proposition which is merely analogous to the point under discussion, but which still lends some support to the statement, conclusion, or opinion presented, use *"cf."* before the citation.

> Cf. Smith v. Abrams, 162 Mo. 220, 140 S.W. 518 (1975) (using cost-benefit analysis to support the construction of additional prisons).

2. *Comparing Authorities With One Another.* To compare one cited case with another case, rather than with the text of the document, use *"Compare . . . with . . . ."*

> Compare Vogel v. Stroh, 205 F.2d 811 (2d Cir. 1975) (holding that an agency's finding of no significant impact under the National Environmental Policy Act could be reviewed solely for procedural defects), with Britton v. Buchanan, 204 F.2d 367 (3d Cir. 1975) (establishing substantive review of agency findings under the National Environmental Policy Act).

3. *Authorities Opposing the Proposition.* When authorities oppose the proposition advanced, various degrees of opposition are indicated by the use of *"but see"* and *"but cf."*

a. *"But see."* The signal *"but see"* precedes a case squarely contradictory to the proposition. It is comparable to *"see."*

> But see Wilson v. Lodge, 245 U.S. 18 (1918) (describing deterrence as the goal of the criminal justice system).

b. *"But cf."*   *"But cf."* is used when citing a case not squarely contradictory to the proposition, but which casts doubt upon it. It is comparable to *"cf."*

> But cf. Areeda v. Steiner, 243 U.S. 21 (1990)
> (refuting the applicability of the benefit
> rule to all damages calculations).

4. *Authority Not Lending Support to Proposition.* When the cited authority is broader in scope than, or develops a question analogous to, discussion in the text without lending support to the proposition asserted, *"see generally"* indicates the cited authority can be profitably compared with the proposition. As with other signals, a parenthetical explanation helps the reader understand the authority's relevance.

> See generally Brylawski, Welfare Systems and
> Poverty in the United States, 68 Yale L.J.
> 812 (1966) (asserting that the welfare system
> is one of several necessary responses to
> poverty in the United States).

5. *Additional Authorities Supporting or Contradicting a Proposition.* Use *"e.g.,"* combined with any signal to indicate that the authority cited is but one of a number of authorities that support or contradict the same proposition. The use of this signal indicates that the cited authority is illustrative, but that citation to additional authorities would not be helpful. This signal should be preceded by a comma when used in combination with other signals (except [no signal]) and is always followed by a comma.

> See, e.g., Gould v. Smith, 212 Mass. 17, 218
> N.E.2d 842 (1965) (clarifying the standard of
> review in summary process cases).

B. ORDER OF AUTHORITIES

Multiple authorities on the same point must be cited in the order set forth below. However, it is seldom wise to give more than two or three authorities for a particular point, unless the authority for your proposition is truly overwhelming.

1. *Order of Signals.* In a citation string, citations are grouped according to the introductory signal preceding them. Each signal or absence of a signal applies to all subsequent citations until another signal is given or the citation sentence ends. Signals are given in the following order. First, signals indicating support. Second, comparative signals. (Note: This does not include *"Cf.,"* which literally means "compare," but which is one of the five signals which are grouped as indicating support.) Third, all signals indicating opposition. Fourth, signals which indicate background material.

The signals in each category must be strung together in one citation sentence. Authorities introduced with [no signal] are authorities "in support" of the proposition, and should be grouped with authorities introduced by supportive signals for the purpose of the citation sentence rule. Basically, signals of different types begin new citation sentences. A single citation sentence only contains authority that is either supporting, opposing, or neither. If both supporting and opposing citations are used, two citation sentences must be written. For a more complete treatment, refer to *The Bluebook*, rules 1.2 and 1.3. Signal groups are given in the following order:

    a. [No signal];

    b. *Accord*;

    c. *See*;

    d. *See also*;

    e. *Cf.*;

    f. *Compare . . . with . . .*;

    g. *But see*;

    h. *But cf.*; and

    i. *See generally*.

The following illustrates the use of introductory signals in citation sentences:

> Fed. R. Civ. P. 9(a); accord N.J.R. Civ. P. 9(a); see Ehrlich v. Grossman, 215 N.E.2d 919 (Mass. 1966); cf. N.Y.R. Civ. Prac. 97 (McKinney 1962). But see Arp v. Grenier, 234 F.2d 425 (5th Cir. 1956) (rule 9(a) invalid); 2 James W. Moore et al., Moore's Federal Practice ¶ 9.02 (2d ed. 1948); cf. Iowa R. Civ. P. 101. See generally Filvoroff v. Wertheimer, [1953] 1 Q.B. 646.

2. Order Within Signals. Within each group of authorities introduced by a particular signal, constitutions are cited first; statutes second; treaties and other international agreements third; cases fourth; legislative materials fifth; administrative and executive materials sixth; resolutions, decisions, and regulations of intergovernmental organizations seventh; records, briefs, and petitions eighth; secondary materials ninth; and cross-references to the author's own material in the current document tenth. *The Bluebook* exhaustively details further subdivisions within each broad category. Refer to rule 1.4, which notes that sometimes, there may be a substance-related reason for diverting from this order.

3. Order of Cases. Counsel should first cite the strongest authority by the most persuasive court. All else being equal, cases are arranged according to the courts issuing the cited opinions. All the United States courts of appeals are treated as one court for this purpose, as are all district courts. Within each court, order is given reverse chronologically, with the most recent decisions first. Additionally, within groups of cases preceded by the same introductory signal, all citations to holdings precede all citations to (1) alternative holdings; (2) concurring or dissenting opinions; and (3) dicta. These latter three classifications are treated as a single group and no special order among them is required.

C. PARENTHETICALS INDICATING WEIGHT AND EXPLANATION

1. Parentheticals Indicating Weight. When a case is cited for material other than a clear non-alternative majority holding, indicate this in parentheses after the date of the case. Thus, always indicate parenthetically (1) dicta; (2) concurring or dissenting opinions; (3) points decided by implication; (4) plurality opinions; and (5) points on which the holding of the court is not clear. Refer to *The Bluebook*, rule 10.6 for additional information.

a. Dicta. If the proposition was not necessary to the decision in that case, it is dictum; this fact must be conveyed. Place the word "dictum" in parentheses at the end of the citation. Additionally, list the page on which the dictum appears, as well as the page on which the case begins.

    Frederick v. Schwarz, 10 Ohio St. 21, 23, 15
    N.E. 359, 360 (1890) (dictum).

b. Concurring or Dissenting Opinions. If a dissenting or concurring opinion is cited, indicate that fact in parentheses at the end of the citation.

    McLaughlin v. Walter, 250 Pa. 206, 218, 195
    A. 417, 425 (1915) (concurring opinion).

Where naming the judge would provide further relevant information regarding the weight of the authority, include her name in the parenthetical.

    Harkness v. Cass, 315 U.S. 419, 480 (1939)
    (Black, J., dissenting).

c. **Points Decided by Implication; Alternative Holdings.**
Where the point for which the case is cited is obtained by
implication, or is an alternative basis for the decision, that fact
should be indicated parenthetically.

> Kambrie v. David, 21 U.S. (8 Wheat.) 22
> (1823) (by implication).

> Hobart v. Parson, 20 Ohio St. 34 (1873)
> (alternative holding).

d. **Plurality Opinions.** If an opinion was joined by only a
plurality of judges, indicate that fact parenthetically.

> Frontiero v. Richardson, 411 U.S. 677 (1973)
> (plurality opinion).

e. **Unclear Holding.** If the holding of a case is not clear,
indicate that fact parenthetically.

> Sacks v. Hart, 325 U.S. 1 (1945) (holding
> unclear).

Additionally, information regarding prior or subsequent history,
memorandum opinions, weight, and multiple dispositions should
be indicated by the use of explanatory phrases, rather than
parentheticals. Refer to *The Bluebook*, rule 10.7 and table T.9 for
further explication.

2. **Explanatory Parentheticals.** Although *The Bluebook* only
suggests the use of explanatory parentheticals with certain
introductory signals, the touchstone of the use of authority for
practitioners is relevance. Therefore, unless the authority you cite
will be explained in greater detail in the text, provide information
regarding the authority's applicability in an explanatory
parenthetical. Without such elaboration, the reader cannot know
whether the authority is factually or legally relevant. Particularly
useful is a brief statement of the facts or a comment on the case that
helps explain the citation.

> See also Smith v. Peterson, 19 P.2d 1455
> (Cal. 1988) (explaining that the benefit rule
> is only applicable to torts in which a
> byproduct of the alleged harm is tangible);
> Greeley v. Jones, 10 Haw. 16 (1959) (joint
> tortfeasors); Begley v. Louis, 18 Vt. 127
> (1864) (common law rule).

Explanatory parentheticals almost always begin with a present
participle; however, a shorter phrase may be substituted where
appropriate. Moreover, you may also choose to quote a portion of

93

the material in the explanatory parenthetical. In that case, the parenthetical should be capitalized where necessary. Refer to *The Bluebook*, rule 1.5.

3. Order of Parentheticals. Parentheticals indicating weight should precede those giving other information.

> Briffaut v. Gelston, 219 Mass. 14, 191 N.E.
> 12 (1923) (by implication) (per curiam)
> ($10,000 verdict not excessive), aff'd, 212
> U.S. 536 (1925).

Explanatory parenthetical phrases come before subsequent history and related authority citations. *See The Bluebook*, rule 1.5.

IV.   Citation of Cases

A. GENERAL RULES OF FORM

1. Parts of the Citation (Order and Form). Parts of a citation are given in the following order and form:

a. Case Name. Names of both parties and the "v." between them are underlined and followed by a comma: Langevoort v. Sidorov, 422 U.S. 483 (1976). The parties' names can be shortened for the purpose of citation. Rules providing for such shortening are listed in subsections (b) and (c) of this part. They depend upon whether the citation appears in a textual sentence or in a citation sentence. In citing administrative decisions, use the full name of the first named private party.

b. Reporter. This part of the citation gives (a) the volume number; (b) the name of the reporter; and (c) the page number in the reporter on which the decision begins.

If the court that rendered the decision is unclear from the reporter name, then the court must be indicated in parentheses with the date at the end of the citation: McDonald v. Cooper, 254 Misc. 498, 50 N.Y.S.2d 891 (N.Y. Sup. Ct. 1959). In this example, the reporter names, *New York Miscellaneous Reports*, and *West's New York Supplement*, do not indicate that the decision was rendered by the New York Superior Court. Therefore, that fact must be indicated parenthetically with the date. You will include the court in most citations. When writing legal memoranda, you cite only to the unofficial regional reporters

for state cases, and thus, must indicate the state court from which the decision emanated parenthetically. *See The Bluebook*, rule 10.3.1(b).

On the other hand, when writing documents to be submitted to the courts of the state that decided the case, you will include a citation to both the official state reporter and the regional reporter. In these instances, you frequently may omit the court indicator from the date parenthetical, because the court will be clear from the title of the official state reporter. *See The Bluebook*, practitioners' note P.3. In all federal cases, other than United States Supreme Court cases, you must indicate either the circuit or the district of the decision. *See The Bluebook*, table T.1.

c. Date. The year of the decision is enclosed in parentheses at the end of the citation. Note that often, the case will be argued in one year and decided the next. Both dates will be given in the reporter. However, the date which must be provided in the citation is the date of the decision, and not the date of argument. For situations in which the date is unclear, refer to *The Bluebook*, rule 10.5.

d. Subsequent and Prior History. Give the subsequent history of a case when you cite the decision in full. However, indicating the denial of a writ of certiorari is optional. Additionally, you may omit the history on remand or denial of a rehearing unless including the information would be helpful to your position. Any disposition of the case which is subsequently "undone" by the deciding authority may also be omitted.

> Donald J. Dietrich, 39 T.C. 271 (1962),
> rev'd, 330 F.2d 985 (6th Cir. 1964); Abrams
> v. Cushing, 101 Mass. 362, 48 N.E. 384
> (1901), aff'd, 200 U.S. 201 (1904);
> Simkowitz v. Wyse, 120 Pa. 381, 43 N.E. 760
> (1911), cert. denied, 98 U.S. 859 (1912).

Refer to *The Bluebook*, rule 10.7.2, regarding the use of different case names in prior or subsequent history.

2. *Omissions in Case Names*

a. Secondary Parties. Names of all parties (except the first listed on each side) and words (such as "et al.") that indicate multiple parties are omitted. See *The Bluebook*, rule 10.2.1(a), for exceptions.

b. Procedural Phrases. *"Ex parte,"* *"In re,"* and other procedural phrases can be omitted when adversary parties are named. *"Ex rel.,"* however, is retained even when adversary parties are named. Refer to *The Bluebook*, rule 10.2.1(b), for further details.

c. Given Names and Initials. Given names and initials of individuals are omitted, but not when they are part of the name of a business firm. Also, do not abbreviate given names where the individual's surname is abbreviated. *See The Bluebook*, rule 10.2.1(g).

d. State Names. "State of," "Commonwealth of," and "People of" are omitted except in citing decisions of the courts of that state. In such cases, only "People," "Commonwealth," or "State" should be retained.

> *Minnesota case cited in a document submitted to a Minnesota court:*
>
> ```
> Seiker v. State, 752 Minn. 43, 545 N.W.2d
> 1205 (1995).
> ```

> *Minnesota case cited in a document submitted to a Massachusetts court:*
>
> ```
> Seiker v. Minnesota, 545 N.W.2d 1205 (1995).
> ```

e. Phrases of Location. Phrases of location (such as "of Boston") are omitted unless they follow "City" (or other similar words) or the omission would leave only one word in the name of a party or corporation. Do not omit such phrases where they designate a national or larger geographical area. *Note*: "of America" is always omitted after "United States."

f. Consolidated Actions. If a case is the consolidation of two or more actions, cite only the first listed.

3. *Abbreviations in Case Names*

a. Commonly Abbreviated Full Names. When the entire name of a party is commonly abbreviated to widely recognized initials, such abbreviation is acceptable in the citation.

b. Abbreviations of Words Within Names. A word which is commonly abbreviated may be shortened in a citation if it is not the first word of the name of a party. In textual sentences, only a limited number of words may be further abbreviated. *See The Bluebook*, rule 10.2.1(c). In citation sentences, further abreiate case names according to *The Bluebook*, rule 10.2.2 and table T.6. Note the odd spacing and punctuation of many of the abbreviations.

B. CITATIONS TO REPORTERS OF FEDERAL CASES

1. Where There is No Official Citation. If for any reason a case does not appear or has not yet appeared in the official reports, cite only the unofficial reporter.

> Jones v. Jones, 256 S. Ct. 209 (1969).

2. Where the Case Has Not Yet Appeared in Any Report. The full texts of United States Supreme Court and other federal court opinions can generally be found very soon after they are rendered in the *United States Law Week*, which should be cited if it is the only available reference.

> Jones v. Mullaney, 26 U.S.L.W. 4416 (U.S. Jan. 7, 1959).

If the opinion does not appear in any report, then the following form may be used:

> Jones v. Jones, Civil No. 51-1250 (D. Mass., filed Mar. 1, 1959).

Additionally, if the case has not been reported but is available through a widely known electronic database, then the database may be cited instead of the slip opinion. Refer to *The Bluebook*, rule 10.8.1(a).

> United States v. Yellow, No. 20-8625XJ, 1996 U.S. App. LEXIS 9020, at *5 (10th Cir. Mar. 12, 1996).

> Times Ahead, Inc. v. United States, No. 39-426Z, 1996 WL 26400 (T.C. Jan. 3, 1996).

C. CITATIONS TO REPORTERS OF STATE CASES

In addition to rules mentioned previously, there are several other points worth mentioning with regard to citation of state cases:

1. Early State Reports. The early state reports were prepared by and listed under the names of individual reporters. The abbreviations for the more commonly cited early reports appear in *The Bluebook*, table T.1. Where the jurisdiction is not shown by such a citation, it should appear in the parentheses with the date.

> Jones v. Doe, 4 Wend. 10 (N.Y. 1835).

> Roe v. Smith, 5 Wend. 13, 12 Am. Dec. 68 (N.Y. 1836).

2. *Exceptional State Reports.* In many jurisdictions the official reporter covers only the decisions of the highest appellate court in the state. The court need not be specifically named where this is the case, since the information regarding the court is conveyed by the name of the report. In other jurisdictions there are several courts reported in a single reporter. There also may be separate official reporters for intermediate courts and courts of last resort. Indicate the particular court from which the decision came unless the court is the highest in the state. If the court is clear from the name of the reporter, the court of decision need not be indicated even though it is not the highest in the state.

> Morris v. Benbassat, 210 P.2d 887 (Cal. 1955).
>
> Fried v. Adler, 28 Ariz. App. 73, 14 P.2d 449 (1951).

A list of all state reporters and the courts they cover can be found in table T.1 of *The Bluebook.*

V.   Citation of Statutes and Constitutions

A. IN GENERAL

1. *Session Laws and Compilations.* Statute reports may roughly be divided into two classes: session laws and compilations. The session laws are usually printed in the chronological order of enactment and are nearly always official reports of the legislature; compilations are usually arranged according to subject matter and may or may not have official status. Because of the large variety of titles which are employed, it is impossible to give a list of both classes for each state and their proper method of citation.

a. Compilations. Cite a state statute only to the latest official statutory compilation, if it appears therein. The official compilations are not always up to date, and they may not include all of the statutes. In the latter event, cite the statute to the unofficial compilation.

> Ill. Rev. Stat. ch. $111\frac{1}{2}$, paras. 35.27–.31 (1963).
>
> Mass. Gen. Laws Ann. ch. 94, § 19 (West 1954).
>
> Tenn. Code Ann. § 8582 (1955).

b. Session Laws. If the statute is contained in neither official nor unofficial compilations, cite it to the session laws.

> 1975 N.Y. Laws 520.

2. General Rules on Form. In contrast to cases, statutes are not underlined or italicized. Statutes are primary authorities and should be listed as such in the Table of Citations. A listing of the statutes cited should precede a listing of the secondary authorities used.

B. FEDERAL STATUTES

1. General Form of Citation. In citing United States statutes enacted into positive law, indicate only the title, section, and date of the code along with the name of the statute if it is commonly cited by that name.

```
Declaratory Judgment Act § 1, 28 U.S.C.
§§ 2201-02 (1959).
```

Refer to *The Bluebook*, rules 12.2.1 and 12.2.2, for the general rule regarding statute citation and its exceptions.

2. Amended Statutes. It may be relevant that the statutory language being cited differs from an earlier or later version of the statute. The following rules indicate how this information, if desired, may be conveyed in the citation.

a. Statutes No Longer in Force. When referring to a statutory section no longer in force, cite that section to the last edition of the official or unofficial code in which the section appeared and provide an official code citation for the current version of the section. Refer to *The Bluebook*, rules 12.2.1(b) and 12.6.1 for further guidance.

```
Clayton Act ch. 25, § 7, 38 Stat. 730 (1914),
amended by 15 U.S.C. § 18 (1964).
```

If discussing the present version:

```
Clayton Act § 7, 15 U.S.C. § 18 (1964),
formerly ch. 25, § 7, 38 Stat. 730 (1914).
```

b. Additions — Statute Still in Force. When citing a statutory section that has been amended by an addition to the former version, cite both versions to the current official code if possible. If discussing the present version:

```
28 U.S.C. § 2201(b) (Supp. I 1965) (amending
28 U.S.C. § 2201 (1964)).
```

If discussing the former version:

```
28 U.S.C. § 2201 (1964), amended by, 28
U.S.C. § 2201(b) (Supp. I 1965).
```

C. STATE STATUTES

1. Official Compilation. Cite state statutes to the latest official compilation; if not contained therein, cite the statute to the preferred unofficial compilation.

> Ill. Rev. Stat. ch. 32, para. 439.50 (1963).
>
> Mass. Gen. Laws ch. 41, § 95 (1932).
>
> N.J. Rev. Stat. § 43:22-5 (Supp. 1955).

2. Unofficial Compilation. If the statute has been amended or enacted subsequent to the most recent supplement to the official compilation, cite the preferred unofficial compilation.

> Pa. Stat. Ann. tit. 2, § 4656.13 (1959).

Refer to *The Bluebook*, table T.1, for statutory compilations, session laws, and administrative materials by jurisdiction.

D. CONSTITUTIONS

Constitutions should precede statutes in any listing (for instance, in the Table of Citations section of the brief), but are cited under the general heading of statutes.

> U.S. Const. art. III, § 8.
>
> U.S. Const. amend. XIV, § 2.
>
> Mont. Const. art. 8, § 16.

The date is given only where a constitution other than the one in force is cited.

> Ga. Const. of 1875, art. II, § 1.

APPENDIX B

Sample Record: *Bell-Wesley v. O'Toole*

SUPERIOR COURT FOR THE STATE OF AMES

REBECCA AND SCOTT BELL-WESLEY,
      Plaintiffs,

                                CIVIL ACTION 96-2004

      v.

                                COMPLAINT

DR. STEPHEN O'TOOLE,
      Defendant.

JURISDICTION

1. Plaintiffs Rebecca and Scott Bell-Wesley are a married couple residing in the State of Ames.

2. Defendant Stephen O'Toole is a medical doctor who resides and has his medical office in the State of Ames.

CAUSES OF ACTION

3. Plaintiff Scott Bell-Wesley is an architect, under employment of the City of Holmes, City Planning Department.

4. Plaintiff Rebecca Bell-Wesley is an attorney, practicing with the Office of the Attorney General of the State of Ames, in the City of Holmes.

5. Prior to January 4, 1996, Plaintiff Rebecca Bell-Wesley had given birth to three deformed children, each of whom had died within six months after birth. Defendant O'Toole informed Plaintiffs that there was a seventy-five percent chance that any child they conceived would suffer and die from the same congenital deformity.

6. Plaintiffs chose to lead a childless lifestyle by procuring a sterilization operation.

7. On October 16, 1993, Defendant performed a vasectomy on Plaintiff Scott Bell-Wesley for the purpose of preventing conception and birth of a child.

8. Defendant O'Toole was solely responsible for the performance of said operation, and for Plaintiff's post-operative care.

9. Plaintiffs were advised by Defendant that the operation would not render Plaintiff Scott Bell-Wesley sterile immediately, and that an alternative means of birth control should be used by Plaintiffs until ten weeks after the operation.

10. Plaintiffs used an alternate method of birth control for three months after Scott Bell-Wesley's vasectomy.

11. Plaintiffs were further informed by Defendant O'Toole that a sperm count would have to be performed twelve to fourteen weeks after the operation in order to determine the success of the operation.

12. Plaintiff Scott Bell-Wesley returned to the office of Defendant O'Toole on January 8, 1994, at which time the Defendant performed a sperm count and informed Plaintiffs that Mr. Bell-Wesley was sterile.

13. Defendant O'Toole determined that Plaintiff Rebecca Bell-Wesley was pregnant on April 20, 1995.

14. Plaintiff Rebecca Bell-Wesley gave birth to Frank Michael Bell on January 4, 1996.

15. Plaintiff Scott Bell-Wesley is the biological father of Frank Michael Bell.

16. Defendant's separate acts of negligence were the proximate causes of the injury suffered by Plaintiffs.

17. Plaintiffs were injured by the birth of their unplanned child.

18. Defendant's negligence has denied Plaintiffs their constitutionally protected right of self-determination in matters of childbearing.

19. Plaintiffs have incurred mental, physical, and financial injuries as a result of the conception and birth of their child, for which Defendant is liable.

2

REMEDY

Wherefore, Plaintiffs pray the Court for the following relief:

20. That Defendant be held liable for the cost of Scott Bell-Wesley's vasectomy, including his medical expenses, his pain and suffering, and Rebecca's loss of consortium during his recuperation period, in the amount of $10,000.

21. That Defendant be held liable for the medical expenses and pain and suffering caused by Rebecca Bell-Wesley's pregnancy and for Scott Bell-Wesley's loss of consortium during the last part of her pregnancy, in the amount of $15,000.

22. That the Defendant be held liable to Plaintiff Rebecca Bell-Wesley for the medical expenses and pain and suffering caused by her giving birth to Frank Michael Bell, in the amount of $25,000.

23. That Defendant be held liable to Plaintiffs for their emotional trauma caused by the conception and birth of an unplanned and unwanted child and for the additional emotional trauma resulting from Plaintiffs' reasonable expectation that the child would suffer from a congenital deformity, in the amount of $100,000.

24. That the Defendant be held liable to Plaintiffs for lost earnings incurred as a result of Rebecca Bell-Wesley's pregnancy and the birth and care of their child, in the amount of $16,000.

25. That the Defendant be held liable to Plaintiffs for injury to Plaintiffs' lifestyle, which is impacted financially by the care and rearing of their child, and for their loss of control over their leisure hours, in the amount of $150,000. (See Exhibit A, attached.)

26. That the Defendant be held liable to Plaintiffs for the financial and emotional cost of rearing their child, in the amount of $250,000.

3

Plaintiffs further pray that the Court order any additional measure of damages as would be just, and that provision for attorney's fees be made.

               Respectfully submitted,

               Scott and Rebecca Bell-Wesley
               by their attorney

               Jane E. Harvey
               Llewellyn, Murray & Silber
               325 North Bridge Road
               Holmes, Ames

4

EXHIBIT A (in part)

From the 1994 annual report by the Department of Health and Human Services, Washington, D.C.

The cost of raising a child, outside of possibly purchasing a home, is the single greatest investment a family will make. Current projections, stipulating that there is virtually no limit on what a couple may invest, indicate that the very minimum parents will spend bringing a child up to majority will be $100,000. This figure includes the basic costs of housing, feeding, and clothing the child, as well as the minimum costs of maintaining his/her health up to age eighteen. Addition of even several moderately priced extras — early professional child care, private schooling, college, allowances for serious illness — can push the cost of childrearing beyond $200,000. And these figures do not yet even contemplate the emotional costs of raising a child.

5

SUPERIOR COURT FOR THE STATE OF AMES

REBECCA AND SCOTT BELL-WESLEY,

       Plaintiffs,

                              CIVIL ACTION 96-2004

       v.

                              DEFENDANT'S ANSWER

DR. STEPHEN O'TOOLE,

       Defendant.

1. Defendant admits the allegations in paragraphs 1-5 of Plaintiffs' Complaint.

2. Defendant denies the allegations in paragraph 6 of Plaintiffs' Complaint.

3. Defendant admits the allegations in paragraphs 7-14 of Plaintiffs' Complaint.

4. Defendant is without sufficient information to respond to paragraph 15 of Plaintiffs' Complaint.

5. Defendant denies the allegations in paragraphs 16-26 of Plaintiffs' Complaint.

FIRST AFFIRMATIVE DEFENSE

6. Plaintiffs assumed the risk of possible failure of the sterilization procedure.

7. Since even perfectly performed vasectomies are not successful in all cases, Plaintiffs assumed the risk of failure of the operation, whether resulting from negligence or regrowth.

6

8. Since the social value of sterilization operations is so high, society has imposed this assumption of risk or waiver of recovery rights for those engaging in a procedure which cannot yet be made 100% effective, regardless of whether negligence was involved.

SECOND AFFIRMATIVE DEFENSE

9. Defendant was not negligent in his operative or post-operative procedures with Plaintiff Scott Bell-Wesley.

10. Plaintiff Scott Bell-Wesley suffered a tubal regrowth which was a statistical failure of the procedure not caused by Defendant's negligence.

THIRD AFFIRMATIVE DEFENSE

11. The birth of a child is always a benefit and a blessing which outweigh any financial costs, as well as any pain and suffering incurred during pregnancy.

12. Where the parents' express purpose in procuring a vasectomy was to prevent the birth of a deformed child, the birth to the parents of a healthy child caused them no injury.

13. Therefore, Plaintiffs did not suffer any damages and Defendant is not liable to Plaintiffs.

FOURTH AFFIRMATIVE DEFENSE

14. Broad social policies prohibit the awarding of child rearing damages in actions for wrongful pregnancy.

7

15. Therefore, Plaintiffs are not entitled to any damages for the cost of raising their child.

FIFTH AFFIRMATIVE DEFENSE

16. Plaintiffs have failed to mitigate the damages claimed in paragraph 23 of their Complaint by refusing, as they have in the past, to undergo amniocentesis, a safe, simple test conducted early in the pregnancy which would have determined that the child being carried was normal and healthy.

17. Plaintiffs have further failed to mitigate the damages in that they have not offered their unwanted, unplanned child up for adoption.

Respectfully submitted,
Dr. Stephen O'Toole
by his attorney

D. Nathan Neuville

D. Nathan Neuville
Ericson, Swanson and Moses
1977 Pond Ave.
Holmes, Ames

8

TRIAL RECORD

(Parts have been omitted)

COUNSEL: Mrs. Bell-Wesley, what happened in the months following the presumably successful sterilization procedure?

REBECCA BELL-WESLEY: Well, shortly after Scott's vasectomy I accepted an offer from the Attorney General to become one of his First Assistant Attorneys General.

COUNSEL: Are there many of these First Assistant Attorneys General?

REBECCA BELL-WESLEY: Oh, no. Just a handful — no more than four or five, each located in a different city in Ames.

COUNSEL: I see, and is more involved in this new position than in your prior position?

REBECCA BELL-WESLEY: Yes, various department heads reported to me. I also had considerable discretion over the policies promulgated by our office, as well as identification of our litigation goals and authorization of compromises and settlements.

COUNSEL: You say "had." Are you no longer in this position?

REBECCA BELL-WESLEY: It's not clear. I have taken a six-month leave of absence, so I should return to work sometime in May. In the meantime, many things could happen. The Attorney General's Office is a political office, you know.

COUNSEL: Was your position as First Assistant Attorney General obtained by political appointment?

REBECCA BELL-WESLEY: No, the Attorney General usually only bothers himself with hiring or bringing in his own first assistants and department chiefs. I was hired out of law school by a department chief at the time.

9

COUNSEL: And what was your salary change upon acceptance of your most recent position?

REBECCA BELL-WESLEY: I went from $48,000 per year to $64,000.

10

SUPERIOR COURT FOR THE STATE OF AMES

REBECCA AND SCOTT BELL-WESLEY,

       Plaintiffs,

                     CIVIL ACTION 96-2004

       v.

                     FINDINGS OF FACT AND
                     CONCLUSIONS OF LAW

DR. STEPHEN O'TOOLE,

       Defendant.

FINDINGS OF FACT

1. Plaintiffs made a conscious decision to avoid the possibility of the conception and birth of a child. The motive for this decision was their fear of having a deformed child.

2. In furtherance of this decision, Plaintiff Scott Bell-Wesley obtained a vasectomy from Dr. O'Toole on October 16, 1993.

3. Expert testimony showed that Defendant failed to sever properly the tubes of the vas deferens, and the Plaintiff Scott Bell-Wesley was never rendered sterile.

4. Defendant negligently performed a sperm count and informed Plaintiffs that Scott Bell-Wesley had been rendered sterile on January 8, 1994.

5. Defendant is a general practitioner medical doctor who has performed vasectomies in his office over the past few years.

6. Plaintiff Rebecca Bell-Wesley conceived a child and bore that child, Frank Michael Bell, on January 4, 1996.

11

7. Scott Bell-Wesley has been established as the biological father. The pregnancy and childbirth were normal and without complications, except that they were unplanned; Frank Michael Bell was born healthy and has remained so.

8. Plaintiffs declined to abort the child on moral grounds, and have declined to give the child up for adoption for personal reasons.

9. Plaintiffs' lifestyle has changed dramatically since the birth of the child.

10. Both parents have lost, and will continue to lose, time and wages in their chosen careers as a result of caring for the child.

11. Both parents profess a deep love for their child even though they bring the present action.

12. Expert testimony established that amniocentesis would have revealed that the fetus was not deformed and was in fact in good health.

CONCLUSIONS OF LAW

1. Defendant Dr. Stephen O'Toole negligently performed a vasectomy on Plaintiff Scott Bell-Wesley on October 16, 1993. The vasectomy was unsuccessful.

2. Defendant O'Toole negligently performed a sperm count on January 8, 1994; informed Plaintiffs that the operation was successful; and told them that Scott Bell-Wesley had been rendered sterile.

3. The conception and birth of Plaintiffs' child would not have resulted had the operation been successful.

4. Plaintiffs have stated a cause of action for negligence.

12

5. Plaintiffs' damages are limited to the out-of-pocket costs, pain and suffering, emotional trauma, lost earnings and loss of consortium associated with Scott Bell-Wesley's vasectomy and Rebecca Bell-Wesley's pregnancy. A reasonable award for these damages is $100,000.

6. Damages are not awardable for the costs associated with rearing a healthy child, because the benefits of a healthy child always outweigh any attendant costs.

DATED: May 13, 1996

NANCY LLEWENSTEIN
Ames Superior Court Judge

13

SUPERIOR COURT OPINION

Llewenstein, J.

In this bench trial, the Court is faced with a difficult problem involving not only the rights of individuals, but also numerous social and systemic considerations. It is apparent that Scott Bell-Wesley's sterilization operation was performed negligently. Not only was the operation itself ineffective, but also, the Defendant was subsequently negligent in performing a sperm count on Plaintiff Scott Bell-Wesley and in informing the Bell-Wesleys, on the basis of this test, that Mr. Bell-Wesley had been rendered sterile.

Plaintiffs allege that the birth of a healthy son must somehow be compensated by the Defendant. The idea that a child would grow up being supported by someone other than his parents by virtue of the fact that his parents did not plan for or want him is extremely disturbing. The very real inability to assign a dollar amount to such an injury is exceeded only by the harm which such an award could do to families and individuals in our society. Perhaps I am old-fashioned, but I believe people are still filled with mystery, joy and inspiration at the birth of a new human life. In this case, where the Plaintiffs' prior conceptions resulted in the births and tragic deaths of three congenitally deformed infants, the birth to them of a healthy child is truly a blessing. The benefits of a healthy child clearly outweigh any and all costs associated with raising the child.

Scott Bell-Wesley's vasectomy was improperly performed and the post-operative care he received was inadequate. The Defendant is liable for his improper medical treatment, and therefore, damages of $100,000 are awarded to Plaintiffs. However, Ames will not join the ranks of jurisdictions recognizing child-rearing costs as an element of damages in a wrongful pregnancy action. The benefits of a healthy child always outweigh any attendant costs or burdens. This case is no different.

14

SUPERIOR COURT FOR THE STATE OF AMES

REBECCA AND SCOTT BELL-WESLEY,

       Plaintiffs,

                             CIVIL ACTION 96-2004

       v.

                             JUDGMENT

DR. STEPHEN O'TOOLE,

       Defendant.

JUDGMENT OF TRIAL COURT

The issues in the above action having duly been heard by this Court, and this Court having made and filed its findings of fact and conclusions of law on May 13, 1996, it is, therefore,

ORDERED, ADJUDGED, AND DECREED, that judgment be entered for Plaintiffs as to Defendant's acts of negligence and Plaintiffs be awarded $100,000 in damages.

DATED: May 20, 1996

John James
          Clerk of Court

15

SUPERIOR COURT FOR THE STATE OF AMES

REBECCA AND SCOTT BELL-WESLEY,

      Plaintiffs,

          CIVIL ACTION 96-2004

      v.

          NOTICE OF APPEAL

DR. STEPHEN O'TOOLE,

      Defendant.

Notice is hereby given that Petitioners, Rebecca and Scott Bell-Wesley, appeal to the Court of Appeals for the State of Ames (N.E. Division), from the final judgment entered in this action on the 13th day of May, 1996.

Dated: May 21, 1996

Jane E. Harvey
Attorney for Appellants
Llewellyn, Murray & Silber
325 North Bridge Road
Holmes, Ames

16

SUPERIOR COURT FOR THE STATE OF AMES

REBECCA AND SCOTT BELL-WESLEY

        Plaintiffs,

                            CIVIL ACTION 96-2004

        v.

                            STIPULATION OF THE RECORD

DR. STEPHEN O'TOOLE,

        Defendant.

It is hereby stipulated by the attorneys for the respective parties in the above-named action, that the following shall constitute the transcript of the record on appeal.

1. Pleadings before the Superior Court of the State of Ames:

    a. Summons (omitted)

    b. Complaint

    c. Exhibit A

    d. Return of Service (omitted)

    e. Answer

    f. Affidavit of Service (omitted)

2. Trial Record

3. Findings of Fact and Conclusions of Law

4. Opinion of the Superior Court of the State of Ames

5. Judgment of the Superior Court of the State of Ames

6. Notice of Appeal

7. This Designation

17

COURT OF APPEALS FOR THE STATE OF AMES
(N.E. DIVISION)

REBECCA AND SCOTT BELL-WESLEY,

      Plaintiffs,

                             Sitting Below:

      v.   Judge Llewenstein

                             CIVIL ACTION 96-2004

DR. STEPHEN O'TOOLE,

      Defendant.

OPINION AFFIRMING THE TRIAL COURT'S
DECISIONS OF LAW

Syllabus: This case arises out of facts centering around the birth of a child. . . .

. . . .

   The Plaintiffs' appeal in this case must be rejected by this Court. We do so largely on the same grounds that led Judge Llewenstein to reject them in the first instance. While we will explain ourselves at length below, we do not wish to imply that our discussion intimates anything but agreement with Judge Llewenstein's views. . . .

18

COURT OF APPEALS FOR THE STATE OF AMES
(N.E. DIVISION)

REBECCA AND SCOTT BELL-WESLEY,

      Plaintiffs,

                               CIVIL ACTION 96-2004

      v.

                               NOTICE OF APPEAL

DR. STEPHEN O'TOOLE,

      Defendant.

    Notice is hereby given that Petitioners, Rebecca and Scott Bell-Wesley, petition for certiorari the Supreme Court of the State of Ames, from the decision of the Court of Appeals for the State of Ames (N.E. Division) in this action on the 13th day of July, 1996.

    Dated: July 21, 1996

                               Jane E. Harvey
                               Attorney for Appellants
                               Llewellyn, Murray & Silber
                               325 North Bridge Road
                               Holmes, Ames

19

IN THE AMES SUPREME COURT

REBECCA AND SCOTT BELL-WESLEY,

              Petitioners,

                  v.

DR. STEPHEN O'TOOLE,

             Respondent.

Sitting Below:

Judge Trimble

Judge Lule

Judge Haentgens
CIVIL ACTION 96-2004

GRANT OF CERTIORARI

This Court hereby grants certiorari on the following issue in the case of <u>Bell-Wesley v. O'Toole</u>:

> Whether the cost of raising a healthy child should properly be included as an element of damages in a wrongful pregnancy action.

Assume that no arguable issue exists concerning:

1. Plaintiffs timeliness in bringing the action under the relevant statute of limitations.

2. Defendant's negligence in performing the operation and in performing the sperm count upon which he relied in informing Plaintiffs that Scott Bell-Wesley was sterile.

3. The actual <u>amount</u> of damages as a goal upon appeal. Quantification and award of each element is determined upon remand; the issue then is whether the court should recognize each type of damage as recoverable.

20

APPENDIX C
Sample Research Pages

ILLUSTRATION #1A
American Law Reports, Quick Index

ALR QUICK INDEX

VARIANCES—Cont'd

Application, zoning board's grant of new application for zone change, variance, or special exception after denial of previous application covering same property or part thereof, 52 ALR3d 494

Cemeteries, 96 ALR3d 921

Comprehensive plan, requirement that zoning variances or exceptions be made in accordance with comprehensive plan, 40 ALR3d 372

Cross-examination of witnesses in hearings before administrative zoning authorities, right to, 27 ALR3d 1304

Fences, zoning regulations prohibiting or limiting fences, hedges, or walls, 1 ALR4th 373

Fraternities or sororities, application of zoning regulations to, 25 ALR3d 921

Funeral homes, construction and application of zoning regulations in connection with funeral homes, 92 ALR3d 328

Highway and traffic changes, authority of zoning commission to impose, as condition of allowance of special exception, permit, or variance, requirements as to highway and traffic changes, 49 ALR3d 492

Hospitals, validity and construction of zoning regulations expressly referring to hospitals, sanitariums, nursing homes, 27 ALR3d 1022

Interim zoning ordinance, validity and effect of, 30 ALR3d 1196

Junkyard, validity, construction, and application of zoning ordinance relating to operation of junkyard or scrap metal processing plant, 50 ALR3d 837

Landlord, rights between landlord and tenant as affected by zoning regulations restricting contemplated use of premises, 37 ALR3d 1018

Minimum lot size requirements, see group Zoning in this topic

Motels or motor courts, application of zoning regulations to, 23 ALR3d 1210

Multiple dwelling, occupation of less than all dwelling units as discontinuance or abandonment of multifamily dwelling nonconforming use, 40 ALR4th 1012

New building or structure, construction on premises devoted to nonconforming use as violation of zoning ordinance, 10 ALR4th 1122

Nonconforming use, construction of new building or structure on premises devoted to nonconforming use as violation of zoning, 10 ALR4th 1122

Notice, construction and application of statute or ordinance provisions requiring notice as prerequisite to granting variance or exception to zoning requirement, 38 ALR3d 167

Other violations, enforcement of zoning regulation affected by, 4 ALR4th 462

Pollution control, validity, construction, and application of variance provisions in state and local air pollution control laws and regulations, 66 ALR4th 711

VARIANCES—Cont'd

Restrictive covenants, what constitutes a family within meaning of zoning regulation or restrictive covenant, 71 ALR3d 693

Sales contracts, zoning or other public restrictions on the use of property as affecting rights and remedies of parties to contract for the sale thereof, 39 ALR3d 362

Standing
- municipal corporation or other governmental body, standing to attack zoning of land lying outside its borders, 49 ALR3d 1126

Zoning
- alteration, extension, reconstruction, or repair of nonconforming structure or structure devoted to nonconforming use as violation of zoning ordinance, 63 ALR4th 275
- laches as defense in suit by governmental entity to enjoin zoning violation, 73 ALR4th 870
- minimum lot size requirements
- - construction and application of zoning laws setting, 2 ALR5th 553
- - validity of zoning laws setting minimum lot size requirements, 1 ALR5th 622
- time, construction and effect of statute requiring that zoning application be treated as approved if not acted on within specified period of time, 66 ALR4th 1012

VARIANCES BETWEEN PLEADINGS AND PROOF

New trial, necessity and propriety of counteraffidavits in opposition to motion for new trial in civil case, 7 ALR3d 1000

Traffic offenses, validity and construction of legislation authorizing revocation or suspension of operator's license for habitual, persistent, or frequent violations of traffic regulations, 48 ALR4th 367

VASCULAR SYSTEM

Damages
- circulatory, digestive, and glandular systems, injuries to, or conditions induced in, 14 ALR4th 539
- organic systems and processes of body, injuries to, 12 ALR4th 475

Insurance
- total or permanent disability within insurance coverage, 21 ALR3d 1383

Lymph System (this index)

Malpractice
generally, 19 ALR3d 825
- catheterization, 31 ALR5th 1, § 3-21
- chiropractors, liability of chiropractors and other drugless practitioners for medical malpractice, 77 ALR4th 273

Total or permanent disability within insurance coverage, 21 ALR3d 1383

VASECTOMIES

Contracts, recovery against physician on basis of breach of contract to achieve particular result or cure, 43 ALR3d 1221

Fraud and deceit
- parent's child support liability as affected by other parent's fraudulent misrepresentation regarding sterility or use of birth control, or refusal to abort pregnancy, 2 ALR5th 337
- sterility or use of birth control, fraud regarding, 31 ALR4th 389
- tort liability, sexual partner's tort liability to other partner for fraudulent misrepresentation regarding sterility or use of birth control resulting in pregnancy, 2 ALR5th 301

Insurance, coverage of artificial insemination procedures or other infertility treatments by health, sickness, or hospitalization insurance, 80 ALR4th 1059

Legitimacy of children, impotency or sterility as rebutting presumption of legitimacy, 84 ALR3d 495

Misrepresentation regarding sterility or use of birth control, 31 ALR4th 389

Support of persons, parent's child support liability as affected by other parent's fraudulent misrepresentation regarding sterility or use of birth control, or refusal to abort pregnancy, 2 ALR5th 337

Tort liability, sexual partner's tort liability to other partner for fraudulent misrepresentation regarding sterility or use of birth control resulting in pregnancy, 2 ALR5th 301

Wrongful birth, tort liability for wrongfully causing one to be born, 83 ALR3d 15

Wrongful conception or pregnancy, recoverability of cost of raising normal, healthy child born as result of physician's negligence or breach of contract or warranty, 89 ALR4th 632

VAULTS

Safes and Vaults (this index)

VCR

Motion pictures and videotapes, applicability of sales or use taxes to, 10 ALR4th 1209

VEGETATION

Billboards, governmental liability for compensation or damages to advertiser arising from obstruction of public view of sign or billboard on account of growth of vegetation in public way, 21 ALR4th 1309

Conservatory for plants, what constitutes incidental or accessory use of property zoned, and primarily used, for residential purposes, 54 ALR4th 1034

Hedges, zoning regulations prohibiting or limiting fences, hedges, or walls, 1 ALR4th 373

For assistance using this Index, call 1-800-527-0430

1229

Permission granted by the copyright holder Lawyers Cooperative Publishing, a division of Thomson Information Services Inc.

ILLUSTRATION #1B
American Law Reports, Volume 89

ANNOTATION

89 ALR4th 632

RECOVERABILITY OF COST OF RAISING NORMAL, HEALTHY CHILD BORN AS RESULT OF PHYSICIAN'S NEGLIGENCE OR BREACH OF CONTRACT OR WARRANTY

by

Russell G. Donaldson, J.D.

TOTAL CLIENT-SERVICE LIBRARY® REFERENCES

61 Am Jur 2d, Physicians, Surgeons, and Other Healers § 282

Annotations: See the related matters listed in the annotation.

1 Ausman & Snyder's Medical Library, L Ed, Gynecology §§ 1:27-1:31

19 Am Jur Pl & Pr Forms (Rev), Physicians, Surgeons, and Other Healers, Forms 296, 297

15 Am Jur Legal Forms 2d, Physicians and Surgeons §§ 202:121-202:131

4 Am Jur Proof of Facts 2d 333, Physician's Guarantee of Medical Results §§ 5, 6-12

L Ed Digest, Physicians and Surgeons § 1

ALR Digest, Abortion § 9; Damages § 138; Physicians and Surgeons § 29.6

Index to Annotations, Abortion; Birth Control; Damages; Fallopian Tube; Malpractice by Medical or Health Professions; Physicians and Surgeons; Sterility and Sterilization; Vasectomies

Auto-Cite®: Cases and annotations referred to herein can be further researched through the Auto-Cite® computer-assisted research service. Use Auto-Cite to check citations for form, parallel references, prior and later history, and annotation references.

Consult POCKET PART in this volume for later cases

ILLUSTRATION #1C
American Law Reports, Volume 89

89 ALR4th   WRONGFUL PREGNANCY DAMAGES
                          89 ALR4th 632

Recoverability of cost of raising normal, healthy child born as result of physician's negligence or breach of contract or warranty

I. PREFATORY MATTERS

§ 1. Introduction
    [a] Scope
    [b] Related matters
§ 2. Summary and comment
    [a] Generally
    [b] Practice pointers

II. GENERAL VIEWS ON RECOVERABILITY

§ 3. View that child-rearing costs not recoverable
§ 4. View that child-rearing costs fully recoverable
§ 5. View that costs recoverable subject to offset for "benefits"
§ 6. —Michigan cases
§ 7. —Minnesota cases

III. PARTICULAR ISSUES IN CONTEXT OF "BENEFITS" RULE

§ 8. Elements of, or factors in determining, "benefits"
§ 9. Cognizability of parents' reasons for avoiding childbirth
§ 10. Mitigation of damages under "avoidable consequences" rule
    [a] Impropriety of considering as militating against any recovery
    [b] Impropriety of considering as not preventing allowance of recovery
    [c] Impropriety waived by plaintiff in "benefits" jurisdiction

---

INDEX

633

ILLUSTRATION #1D
American Law Reports, Volume 89

§ 2[b]   Wrongful Pregnancy Damages   89 ALR4th
89 ALR4th 632

counterargument that where the additional child's birth was sought to be prevented for economic reasons, an unplanned child would be likely to learn this fact at some time in any event, even absent an award of child-rearing expenses, perhaps at a moment of parental frustration, so that a greater threat to love and to corresponding emotional security for an unplanned child, as well as for the other children in the family, would be posed by parental inability to make ends meet than the situation provided when family finances had been stabilized through appropriate compensation for negligence, thus suggesting that the nonaward of child-rearing expenses might be more contributory to emotional insecurity than protective against it.[10]

In a jurisdiction allowing recovery for child-rearing expenses in a "wrongful pregnancy" case under the "benefits" rule offsetting such damages by the benefits to be derived by the parents from the existence of the child's life where the child born is normal and healthy, counsel should note that at least one court has specifically held that the burden of proof in such an action as to the offsetting benefits to be so considered is on the defendant.[11]

On the issue of distribution of damages for child-rearing expenses where allowable, counsel may wish to note that at least one court, adhering to the "benefits" rule, has

indicated, especially where the burden of raising the child in question does not fall on the child's biological parents, but for economic and sociological reasons falls on other family members, that, in order to safeguard the proper use of the recovery for the raising of the child, such funds should be placed in trust for the child's care.[12]

While a number of courts dealing with the measure and elements of damages in "wrongful pregnancy" cases have addressed the issue of mitigation of damages by "abortion or adoption," generally adhering to a view that such issues should not be triable for reasons of public policy or parent-child psychology (§ 10), it is submitted that in a jurisdiction recognizing a tort cause of action but limiting recovery to matters directly connected to the pregnancy and childbirth, so as to deny recovery for costs of raising the child, the question of mitigation of damages would be limited to abortion in any event, since adoption could mitigate only such damages as would relate to the raising of a child already born, and in connection with which the parents would already have suffered all possible recoverable damages.

II. General Views on Recoverability

§ 3. View that child-rearing costs not recoverable

In the following cases involving

---

10. Flowers v District of Columbia (1984, **Dist Col** App) 478 A2d 1073 (Ferren, Associate Judge, in dissent).

11. Morris v Frudenfeld (1982, 2nd

Dist) 135 **Cal** App 3d 23, 185 Cal Rptr 76.

12. Clapham v Yanga (1980) 102 **Mich** App 47, 300 NW2d 727, app dismd (Mich) 335 NW2d 1.

640

Permission granted by the copyright holder Lawyers Cooperative Publishing, a division of Thomson Information Services Inc.

ILLUSTRATION #1E
American Law Reports, Volume 89

89 ALR4th   WRONGFUL PREGNANCY DAMAGES   § 3
89 ALR4th 632

actions for damages arising out of the birth of a healthy, normal child as a result of alleged medical malpractice in abortion, sterilization, or birth control, or as the result of a breach of a contract to achieve either temporary infertility or permanent sterility, the courts held or recognized the view that even if such an action is cognizable in itself, damages therein may never be recovered for the cost of rearing and educating such child to majority.

US—For federal case involving state law, see state headings.

Ala—Boone v Mullendore (1982, Ala) 416 So 2d 718.

Ark—Wilbur v Kerr (1982) 275 Ark 239, 628 SW2d 568.

Del—Coleman v Garrison (1975, Del Sup) 349 A2d 8 (ovrld on other gr by Garrison v Medical Center of Delaware, Inc. (Del Sup) 1989 Del LEXIS 476).[13]

DC—Flowers v District of Columbia (1984, Dist Col App) 478 A2d 1073.[14]

Fla—Fassoulas v Ramey (1984, Fla) 450 So 2d 822.

Public Health Trust v Brown (1980, Fla App D3) 388 So 2d 1084, petition den (Fla) 399 So 2d 1140.

Bradian v Baliton (1979, 19th Cir Ct) 48 Fla Supp 201.

Ga—Fulton-De Kalb Hospital Authority v Graves (1984) 252 Ga 441, 314 SE2d 653.

Blash v Glisson (1984) 173 Ga App 104, 325 SE2d 607.

White v United States (1981, DC

---

13. The latter "Garrison" Case, apparently involving a wholly different set of parties despite the similarity in names, dealt with a question of damages sought as the result of the unwanted birth of a child with Down's Syndrome. In holding that the cost of raising such child, over and above those involved in the raising of a normal, healthy child, the court declared that the earlier case of Coleman v Garrison, which involved a normal, healthy child, was overruled to the extent that it was inconsistent with the holding of the case then at bar, thereby apparently referring to language in the Coleman Case which might imply a view that the birth of any child, in whatever physical or mental condition, would be a blessing outweighing as a matter of law the expenses of raising it. It is thus presumed that the case of Coleman v Garrison cited above remains valid precedent for a proposition that the expenses of raising a normal, healthy child are not recoverable in an action for damages based on the undesired birth of such child.

14. In the earlier case of Hartke v McKelway (1983) 228 App DC 139, 707 F2d 1544, cert den 464 US 983, 78 L Ed 2d 360, 104 S Ct 425 (applying District of Columbia law), the court had determined that, under District of Columbia law as surmised in the absence of existing authority, child-rearing expenses might be recoverable in a proper case, although in the case at bar, wherein the mother's sole reason for seeking sterilization was her fear of complication and possible death to herself as the result of pregnancy, rather than any economic necessity, eugenic consideration, or psychological aversion to parenthood, the court ruled that, as a matter of law under the circumstances made clear by the testimony at trial, the birth in the case at bar was a net benefit to the plaintiff, who therefore should not recover for child-rearing expenses.

641

ILLUSTRATION #2A
Minnesota Statutes Annotated, General Index

WRITS

WRITS—Cont'd
Mandamus, generally, this index
Ne exeat, power of district court to issue, 484.03
Prohibition, generally, this index
Restitution.   Forcible Entry and Detainer, this index
Return, time for, 484.04
Seal, 484.04
Sheriffs, this index
Signing, 484.04
Testing writs, 484.04
Vacancy in office of judge not to abate or discontinue writs, 484.32
Workers' compensation, issuance, 175.101

WRITS OF MANDAMUS
Revisor of statutes, confidential information, 3C.05

WRITTEN
Defined, commercial code, 336.1–201

WRITTEN INSTRUMENTS
Anatomical Gift Act, 525.921 et seq.
International will, requirement, 524.2–1003
Letters of credit, 336.5–104
Sales, this index
Statute of frauds, 513.01 et seq.

WRONGFUL APPROPRIATION
Military justice code, 192A.595

WRONGFUL DEATH
Death, this index

WRONGFUL DEATH ACT
Generally, 573.02

WRONGFUL LIFE AND BIRTH
Actions and proceedings, 145.424

ILLUSTRATION #2B
Minnesota Statutes Annotated

§ 145.423   **PUBLIC HEALTH**

Library References
Abortion and Birth Control ⇐1.
C.J.S. Abortion and Birth Control; Family
   Planning §§ 2 to 9.

145.424. Prohibition of tort actions

Subdivision 1. Wrongful life action prohibited. No person shall maintain a cause of action or receive an award of damages on behalf of that person based on the claim that but for the negligent conduct of another, the person would have been aborted.

Subd. 2. Wrongful birth action prohibited. No person shall maintain a cause of action or receive an award of damages on the claim that but for the negligent conduct of another, a child would have been aborted.

Subd. 3. Failure or refusal to prevent a live birth. Nothing in this section shall be construed to preclude a cause of action for intentional or negligent malpractice or any other action arising in tort based on the failure of a contraceptive method or sterilization procedure or on a claim that, but for the negligent conduct of another, tests or treatment would have been provided or would have been provided properly which would have made possible the prevention, cure, or amelioration of any disease, defect, deficiency, or handicap; provided, however, that abortion shall not have been deemed to prevent, cure, or ameliorate any disease, defect, deficiency, or handicap. The failure or refusal of any person to perform or have an abortion shall not be a defense in any action, nor shall that failure or refusal be considered in awarding damages or in imposing a penalty in any action.
Laws 1982, c. 521, § 1. Amended by Laws 1986, c. 444.

Historical Note
Laws 1986, c. 444, authorized the removal of nonsubstantive gender specific references.

Law Review Commentaries
Surrogate parenthood. 1986, 12 Wm.Mitch-ell L.Rev. 143.

Library References
Abortion and Birth Control ⇐16.
C.J.S. Abortion and Birth Control; Family
   Planning § 4.

Notes of Decisions
Validity 1

___

1. Validity

   Subdivision 2 of this section prohibiting wrongful birth actions did not violate due process or equal protection. Hickman v. Group Health Plan, Inc., 1986, 396 N.W.2d 10.

   Subdivision 2 of this section did not violate section of Minnesota Constitution assuring remedies for rights that vested at common law. Hickman v. Group Health Plan, Inc., 1986, 396 N.W.2d 10.

262

ILLUSTRATION #3A
Ninth Decennial Digest, Part 2, Descriptive Word Index

43–9th D Pt 2—795   VASECTOMY

VALUE—Cont'd
IMPROVEMENTS—
Damages for breach of covenant of warranty. **Covenants 130(6)**
Recovery for breach of covenant of seisin. **Covenants 125(5)**
INCHOATE right of dower. **Dower & C 32**
INCOME tax, see this index Income Tax
INDICTMENT or information—
Allegation as to value—
Of embezzled property. **Embez 29**
Of personal property. **Ind & Inf 104**
Of property stolen. **Rec S Goods 7(5)**
Bribe. **Brib 6(3)**
Variance between allegations and proof. **Ind & Inf 181**
INSURANCE—
Avoidance for misrepresentation, breach of warranty or condition. **Insurance 281**
Forfeiture for breach of warranty, see this index Forfeitures
Limitation of liability as to value or property destroyed. **Insurance 498–500**
Marine insurance. **Insurance 473–475**
Part of value. **Insurance 501**
INTERNAL Revenue, see this index Internal Revenue
INTOXICATING liquors, recovery. **Int Liq 328**
JUDICIAL notice—
Crim Law 304(19)
Evid 18
JURISDICTION affected by amount or value in controversy, see this index Jurisdictional Amount
LACHES affected by change of value. **Equity 72(4)**
LAND sold under contract, see this index Vendor and Purchaser
LAND taken for public use, see this index Eminent Domain
MECHANICS' liens—
Evidence in proceeding to enforce lien. **Mech Liens 280(2)**
Limitation of amount of lien to reasonable value of labor or materials. **Mech Liens 161(3)**
Right to lien affected by. **Mech Liens 54**
OPINION evidence, see this index Opinion Evidence
PLEADING and proof as to value. **Damag 159(8)**
PRINCIPAL and agent, notice to agent of facts affecting value. **Princ & A 177(4)**
PUBLIC service companies, regulation of charges by commission. **Pub Ut 124, 126**
RENT, see this index Rent
REPLEVINED property—
Affidavit. **Replev 30**
Allegation of value in pleading. **Replev 59**
Depreciation in value as element of damages. **Replev 78**
Judgment for value. **Replev 103, 106**
Verdict and findings. **Replev 96**
Writ of replevin. **Replev 37**
ROBBERY, see this index Robbery
SALES, see this index Sales
SERVICES, see this index Services
SLANDER of. **Libel 133**

VALUE—Cont'd
STOLEN property—
Burg 41(7)
Larc 6, 31, 46, 59, 72, 83
Rec S Goods 2, 7(5)
TAXATION—
According to value. **Tax 49**
Tax shelter valuation. **Tax 348(2)**
Apartment house—
Under income-capitalization approach. **Tax 349(5)**
Exemption. **Tax 212**
"Fullest extent possible" standard. **Tax 348.1(1)**
Property of cooperative housing corporation. **Tax 348.1(1)**
Tenants' improvements taxable to owners of shopping center. **Tax 79**
Whether rendered worthless by toxic waste in soil—
Evidence. **Tax 485(3)**
TROVER and conversion, see this index Trover and Conversion
WATCHES—
Evidence of—
Price affixed to by seller. **Evid 113(1)**

VALUED POLICIES
MARINE insurance. **Insurance 475**
PROPERTY or title, extent of loss and liability. **Insurance 500**

VAN
APPLICABILITY of statute relating to operation of vehicles with passengers under age of five. **Autos 148**

VANDALISM
See generally, this index Malicious Mischief
INSTRUCTION on related offense of—
Failure to give—
In burglary prosecution. **Crim Law 795(1)**

VARIANCE
AIR pollution. **Health & E 25.6(7)**
ATTACHMENT, see this index Attachment
AWARD of arbitrators to submission. **Arbit 57–57.3**
CERTIFICATE or declaratory statement of mining location or claim, variation of description from ground marks. **Mines 21(2)**
EMINENT domain, see this index Eminent Domain
INDORSEMENTS and signatures. **Forg 34(3)**
INTERNAL Revenue, see this index Internal Revenue
ISSUES, proof and variance relating thereto, see this index Issues, Proof and Variance
JUDGMENT—
Amendment or correction. **Judgm 305**
Amount of recovery. **Judgm 256(6)**
Attorney's fee. **Judgm 256(7)**
Costs. **Judgm 256(7)**
Findings, conformity of judgment. **Judgm 256**
Grounds of action or defense. **Judgm 250**
Interest. **Judgm 256(7)**

VARIANCE—Cont'd
JUDGMENT—Cont'd
Parties, conformity of judgment to verdict and findings. **Judgm 256(5)**
Pleadings, default judgment. **Judgm 117**
Process, pleadings, proofs, verdict or findings. **Judgm 246–258**
Referee's report. **Judgm 257**
Special verdict and finding. **Judgm 256(2)**
Surplusage in verdict or findings. **Judgm 256(3)**
Verdict and finding. **Judgm 256**
MUNICIPAL improvements—
Notice or petition and ordinance and order. **Mun Corp 304(12)**
Preliminary and final estimates. **Mun Corp 462**
Preliminary resolution or estimate of cost and ordinance and order. **Mun Corp 304(13)**
NOTICE and claim for injury from defect or obstruction in street and pleading or proof. **Mun Corp 816(11)**
OFFER to buy and acceptance. **Sales 23(4)**
OFFER to sell and acceptance. **Sales 22(4)**
PLEADING—
Bill of particulars and pleading. **Plead 328**
Ground for objections to evidence. **Plead 429**
Declaration and process. **Plead 74**
Ground for abatement. **Abate & R 31**
Implied and constructive contracts. **Impl & C C 83**
Pleading and instrument annexed, filed, or referred to. **Plead 312**
Statement and process. **Plead 74**
PLEADING and proof—
See this index Issues, Proof and Variance
Judgment, bar or estoppel, see this index Conclusiveness of Judgments and Decrees
PUBLIC officers and employees—
Disciplinary proceedings—
Notice or charge. **Offic 72.13**
SIGN—
Area variance. **Zoning 503**
TAX deed and prior tax proceedings as to description of property. **Tax 764(3)**
WATER pollution. **Health & E 25.7(16)**
ZONING, see this index Zoning

VARIANCES OR EXCEPTIONS
ZONING, see this index Zoning

"VASCAR" COMPUTER-RECORDER
PRESUMPTION of accuracy—
To speed reading taken by. **Crim Law 388**

VASCULAR INJURY
WORKERS' compensation, accidental injury. **Work Comp 588**

VASECTOMY
PHYSICIAN—
Duty to disclose to patient material risks of complications. **Phys 15(8)**
PHYSICIAN'S negligence resulting in birth of unwanted child, damages. **Phys 18.110**

Ninth Decennial Digest, Part 2, 1981–1986, Descriptive Word Index, page 795
© Copyright 1988 by West Publishing Co. Reprinted with permission.

ILLUSTRATION #3B
Ninth Decennial Digest, Part 2, 1981-1986

⬤18.110 **PHYSICIANS & SURGEONS**   33 9th D Pt 2—968

normal, woman and her husband had no claim for physical pain, suffering and mental anguish of woman which arose from her pregnancy and giving birth.—Id.

In action brought by parents against various physicians specializing in obstetrics and gynecology, their professional association, and their insurance carrier, based on alleged failure of physicians to diagnose and or warn of inheritable disease which resulted in birth of deformed child, parents pled legal cause of action for recovery of medical expenses for extraordinary care involved in treatment of their son due to physical abnormalities which were in excess of cost of raising normal child.—Id.

Ga. 1984. Recovery of expenses for unsuccessful medical procedure which lead to conception or pregnancy, for pain and suffering, medical complications, costs of delivery, lost wages, and loss of consortium are recoverable in an action for wrongful pregnancy or wrongful conception.—Fulton-DeKalb Hosp. Authority v. Graves, 314 S.E.2d 653, 252 Ga. 441.

Costs of raising a child cannot be recovered in action for wrongful pregnancy or wrongful conception.—Id.

Ga.App. 1985. Cause of action for breach of warranty did not exist against doctor who performed sterilization procedure following which plaintiff endured ectopic pregnancy, where patient executed consent form which provided that operation was not guaranteed as to sterility.—Nelson v. Parrott, 333 S.E.2d 101, 175 Ga.App. 307, certiorari denied.

Ga.App. 1984. Even if child was born healthy, claim may be brought against physician for negligent performance of sterilization procedure which resulted in unplanned pregnancy and birth.—Blash v. Glisson, 325 S.E.2d 607.

In action based upon negligent performance of sterilization procedure which resulted in unplanned pregnancy and birth, damages of older children in having to share family income with another individual was not recoverable.—Id.

In action based upon negligent performance of sterilization procedure which resulted in unplanned pregnancy and birth, expenses of unsuccessful medical procedure which led to conception or pregnancy, for pain and suffering, medical complications, costs of delivery, lost wages, and loss of consortium could be recoverable.—Id.

Idaho 1984. Claim for wrongful birth must satisfy the traditional requirements for a negligence action: duty, breach, proximate cause and damages.—Blake v. Cruz, 698 P.2d 315, 108 Idaho 253.

The requisite injury in a wrongful birth claim is the birth of a child, and element of proximate cause is established by showing that, but for physician's negligence, parents would have terminated pregnancy or avoided conception.—Id.

Damages recoverable by parents for wrongful birth of deformed or defective child who would have been aborted or not conceived but for physician's negligence include costs of medical and hospital care and damages for emotional distress, and in case of child who will be relatively helpless and dependent on parents for the duration of its life, expenses for support and maintenance of child beyond the age of majority are recoverable by the parents, while in determining damages for emotional injury, countervailing emotional benefits attributable to the birth of the child should be considered. I.C. §§ 5-311, 32-1002.—Id.

Cause of action for wrongful life, brought by an infant alleging that, due to negligence of defendant physician, birth occurred, is not recognized, even though child is born with birth defects.—Id.

Ill. 1983. Existence of normal, healthy life is esteemed right under law, rather than compensable wrong, and such reasoning is applicable where action is brought for negligent sterilization or negligent failure to determine pregnancy.—Cockrum v. Baumgartner, 69 Ill.Dec. 168, 447 N.E.2d 385, 95 Ill.2d 193, certiorari denied Raja v. Michael Reese Hospital, 104 S.Ct. 149, 464 U.S. 846, 78 L.Ed.2d 139.

Child-rearing costs were not recoverable in action for negligent sterilization or negligent failure to determine pregnancy.—Id.

Ill.App. 1 Dist. 1985. Average life expectancy of 63.3 years of person age 7½ was not conclusive in determining damages to be awarded mentally retarded child in medical malpractice action, but could be considered by jury in connection with other evidence relating to probable life expectancy of particular child, bearing in mind some persons live longer and some persons less than average, and instruction to that effect left room for jury to exercise its right to consider all evidence in light of its own observations and experience in affairs of life and permitted jury to consider evidence that child's lifespan might be less than that of normal person.—Northern Trust Co. v. County of Cook, 90 Ill.Dec. 157, 481 N.E.2d 957, 135 Ill.App.3d 329, appeal denied.

Ill.App. 1 Dist. 1984. To extent that recognition of causes of action for wrongful life or wrongful birth would merely be extension of existing principles of tort law to new factual situations, Appellate Court can and should recognize them.—Goldberg By and Through Goldberg v. Ruskin, 84 Ill.Dec. 1, 471 N.E.2d 530, 128 Ill.App.3d 1029, appeal allowed, affirmed 101 Ill.Dec. 818, 499 N.E.2d 406, 113 Ill.2d 482.

Assuming that physician and his employer owed duty to plaintiff in utero to inform his parents of risk of Tay-Sachs disease and testing procedure for such disease and that defendants' breach of such duty was proximate cause of plaintiff's birth, plaintiff nevertheless failed to state cause of action for wrongful life, in view of apparent absence of legally cognizable injury and impossibility of making comparison required by a compensatory remedy.—Id.

Parents of child born with Tay-Sachs disease, who alleged existence of duty on part of physician and his employer to inform them of risk of such disease and availability of testing procedure for such disease and that breach of duty was proximate cause of child's birth stated cause of action in tort for wrongful birth.—Id.

Extraordinary costs of caring for child born with Tay-Sachs disease were not within definition of "economic loss" so as to be precluded from recovery in negligence action against physician who treated mother during pregnancy.—Id.

Ill.App. 2 Dist. 1985. In husband's malpractice action against social worker, who had sexual relations with wife during course of marital counseling sought by husband and wife, husband would be entitled to recover actual damages, including loss of consortium.—Horak v. Biris, 85 Ill.Dec. 599, 474 N.E.2d 13, 130 Ill.App.3d 140.

Ill.App. 5 Dist. 1986. Trial court in medical malpractice action against pharmacy, doctor, and clinic erred in entering a judgment against pharmacy in amount of $1,689,641 reduced by 15% for the contributory negligence of plaintiff and a judgment against doctor and clinic in the amount of $1,689,641; jury intended to establish one joint and several damage award in the amount of $1,689,641, considering plaintiff's own theory of the case, instructions given to jury, and identical form of assessment of damages.—Fultz v. Peart, 98 Ill.Dec. 285, 494 N.E.2d 212, 144 Ill.App.3d 364, appeal denied.

Ill.App. 5 Dist. 1985. Evidence of patient's medical expenses and lost earnings supported trial court's determination, on patient's motion

for new trial on issue of damages following verdict of $32,500 for patient in his medical malpractice action, that damages awarded to patient were inadequate and warranted new trial on all issues of damages.—Greco v. Coleman, 92 Ill.Dec. 875, 485 N.E.2d 1118, 138 Ill.App.3d 317, appeal denied.

Ill.App. 1982. Though substantial verdict was based almost entirely upon presumption of pecuniary loss, award of $125,000 for loss of unborn fetus was not shown to be excessive. S.H.A. ch. 70, ¶¶ 1-2.2.—Jones v. Karraker, 64 Ill.Dec. 868, 440 N.E.2d 420, 109 Ill.App.3d 363, affirmed 75 Ill.Dec. 233, 457 N.E.2d 23, 98 Ill.2d 487.

Ill.App. 1982. Costs of rearing unplanned child to majority are damages which proximately flow from either tort of medical negligence or breach of contract by physician who fails to properly perform vasectomy, and in assessing damages, jury should be allowed to consider potential benefits of unplanned child which may accrue to family interests.—Pierce v. De Gracia, 59 Ill.Dec. 267, 431 N.E.2d 768, 103 Ill.App.3d 511, reversed 71 Ill.Dec. 893, 451 N.E.2d 1260, 92 Ill.2d 572.

In action against physician for breach of contract and for medical negligence in performing vasectomy, trial court erred in disallowing recovery of costs of raising to majority child born after operation since costs of rearing unplanned child were damages which proximately flowed from physician's negligence or breach of contract.—Id.

Ill.App. 1981. Regardless of motivation, couple has right, which is legally protectible, to determine whether couple will have child; allowance of rearing costs as element of damages arising out of negligently performed sterilization operation is not aspersion upon value of child's life, but, rather, is recognition of importance of parent's fundamental right to control their reproductivity.—Cockrum v. Baumgartner, 54 Ill. Dec. 751, 425 N.E.2d 968, 99 Ill.App.3d 271, reversed 69 Ill.Dec. 168, 447 N.E.2d 385, 95 Ill.2d 193, certiorari denied Raja v. Michael Reese Hospital, 104 S.Ct. 149, 464 U.S. 846, 78 L.Ed.2d 139.

Cost of raising and educating unplanned child is proper element of damages in action brought for negligent performance of sterilization operation.—Id.

Ind.App. 3 Dist. 1985. Damages recoverable in "wrongful pregnancy action" are damages owing parent, not unplanned child, due to unsuccessful medical procedures for sterilization and resulting birth of child.—Garrison v. Foy, 486 N.E.2d 5, rehearing denied.

Limitation of liability is policy of state regarding medical malpractice actions. IC 16-9.5-1-1 et seq.(1982 Ed.).—Id.

Costs of rearing child born after unsuccessful sterilization procedure could not be recovered from health care provider in wrongful pregnancy action. IC 16-9.5-1-1 et seq., 16-10-3-4, 34-1-1-8 (1982 Ed.); IC 34-4-33-1 et seq. (1985 Supp.).—Id.

Exceptional expenses associated with child's bilateral cleft of the lip, jaw and palate were not recoverable in wrongful pregnancy action, where deformity of child was not reasonably foreseeable result of unsuccessful vasectomy.—Id.

Possible damages recoverable in wrongful pregnancy are limited to damages directly caused by unsuccessful sterilization and resultant pregnancy.—Id.

Ind.App. 1982. Although damages from aggravation of injury might not be fully ascertainable because of infant's age, fact that aggravation occurred because of delay in treatment of fracture of infant's femur had to be shown before cause of action in malpractice existed

For references to other topics, see Descriptive-Word Index

ILLUSTRATION #4A
North Eastern Reporter, Second Series, Volume 47

COCKRUM v. BAUMGARTNER   Ill. **385**

Cite as 447 N.E.2d 385 (Ill. 1983)

der of Charles Biebel if the verdict in this case were based on felony murder, a possibility which the evidence and the jury verdict clearly leave open. The majority opinion acknowledges that the evidence indicates that the defendant was not the triggerman in the Biebel murder and that he was engaged in taking stolen items out of the Biebel house to his car when the murder was actually committed. It observes, however, that the *Enmund* decision permits capital punishment where a defendant convicted of felony murder "contemplated" that life would be taken (458 U.S. ——, ——, 102 S.Ct. 3368, 3379, 73 L.Ed.2d 1140, 1154), and proceeds that on the theory that the defendant must have so contemplated in this case because the Mueller murder had occurred earlier under similar circumstances. That is too artful a use of the word "contemplate" in deciding whether a defendant is excluded from the protection of *Enmund,* and is a departure from the *Enmund* holding that the eighth amendment forbids imposition of the death penalty on one "who aids and abets a felony in the course of which a murder is committed by others but who does not himself kill, attempt to kill, or intend that a killing take place or that lethal force will be employed." 458 U.S. ——, ——, 102 S.Ct. 3368, 3376–77, 73 L.Ed.2d 1140, 1151.

Neither a burglary nor the act of carrying stolen items out of a house that is being burglarized is in itself a murderous act. Such conduct by itself does not intimate an intent to kill. That a murder occurred while defendant was carrying items out of a house on a previous occasion may be enough to convey notice to defendant that his accomplice has murderous tendencies, so that a second murder might be said to be *foreseeable* should defendant engage in similar conduct in a subsequent burglary. He would then be liable for the tort of wrongful death as well as for the crime of felony murder. But foreseeability is not the same as intent, active contemplation, or actual anticipation. To equate the concepts, as the majority does, is to read into negligent or reckless conduct a volitional element that does not exist. Basing an

447 N.E.2d—10

execution on so expansive a definition of the word "contemplate" not only does violence to the clear holding of *Enmund* that a person convicted of felony murder cannot constitutionally be put to death absent a showing that he intended that life be taken, but ignores the fact that our criminal code specifically distinguishes "intent" (Ill.Rev. Stat.1979, ch. 38, par. 4–4) from "knowledge" (Ill.Rev.Stat.1979, ch. 38, par. 4–5), "recklessness" (Ill.Rev.Stat.1979, ch. 38, par. 4–6), "negligence" (Ill.Rev.Stat.1979, ch. 38, par. 4–7), and other states of mind and requires, in order to impose a death sentence, that a defendant convicted of felony murder intend to kill or at least know that as a consequence of his actions a death is likely to occur (Ill.Rev.Stat.1979, ch. 38, par. 9–1(b)(6)(b)). I conclude that it is error for the trial court or this court to treat bare foreseeability of the possibility of a death as satisfying the requirements of both *Enmund* and our capital punishment statute that a defendant actually intend a killing or knowingly acquiesce in one.

95 Ill.2d 193
69 Ill.Dec. 168
Donna COCKRUM et al., Appellees,

v.

George BAUMGARTNER et al., Appellants.

Edna RAJA et al., Appellees,

v.

A. TULSKY et al. (Michael Reese Hospital and Medical Center, Appellant).

No. 55733.

Supreme Court of Illinois.

Feb. 18, 1983.

Rehearing Denied April 8, 1983.

In malpractice actions based on so-called "wrongful pregnancy" or "wrongful

ILLUSTRATION #4B
North Eastern Reporter, Second Series, Volume 47

386 Ill.   447 NORTH EASTERN REPORTER, 2d SERIES

birth," counts were dismissed insofar as they set out claims for the expenses of rearing the children. The cases were consolidated on appeal, and the Appellate Court, First District, Fourth Division, reversed and remanded, 99 Ill.App.3d 271, 54 Ill.Dec. 751, 425 N.E.2d 968. Leave was granted to defendants to appeal. The Supreme Court, Ward, J., held that: (1) existence of normal, healthy life is esteemed right under law, rather than compensable wrong, and such reasoning is applicable where action is brought for negligent sterilization or negligent failure to determine pregnancy, and (2) child-rearing costs were not recoverable in action for negligent sterilization or negligent failure to determine pregnancy.

Appellate court reversed; circuit court affirmed.

Clark, J., dissented and filed opinion, in which Simon, J., joined.

---

1. Physicians and Surgeons ⊕=18.110

Existence of normal, healthy life is esteemed right under law, rather than compensable wrong, and such reasoning is applicable where action is brought for negligent sterilization or negligent failure to determine pregnancy.

2. Physicians and Surgeons ⊕=18.110

Child-rearing costs were not recoverable in action for negligent sterilization or negligent failure to determine pregnancy.

Hinshaw, Culbertson, Moelmann, Hoban & Fuller, Chicago, for appellant, Dr. George Baumgartner; Stanley J. Davidson, E. Michael Kelly, Michael R. Goldman, Chicago, of counsel.

Lord, Bissell & Brook, Chicago, for appellant, Michael Reese Hosp. and Medical Center; Harold L. Jacobson, Robert B. Austin, Paul A. Brady, Hugh C. Griffin, Chicago, of counsel.

Ash, Anos, Freedman & Logan, Addis & Brenner Limited, Chicago, for appellees Edna Raja and Afzal Raja; Lawrence M. Freedman, Sheldon A. Brenner, James L. Glass, Jr., Chicago, of counsel.

Kenneth L. Cunniff, Chicago, Keith L. West, Mundelein, for appellees; Jean A. Hellman, Evanston, of counsel.

WARD, Justice:

This appeal concerns the extent of the damages that may be recovered in a malpractice action based on a so-called "wrongful pregnancy" or "wrongful birth." The issue was raised in two medical malpractice suits that were consolidated on appeal from the circuit court of Cook County to the appellate court. In both cases, the plaintiffs had alleged that but for the negligence of the defendants each of the female plaintiffs would not have borne a child. In both actions, the plaintiffs sought to recover for the pain of childbirth, the time lost in having the child, and the medical expenses involved. The plaintiffs sought also to recover as damages the future expenses of raising the children, who, it would appear, are healthy and normal. The circuit court dismissed the counts that set out the claims for the expenses of rearing the children. The plaintiffs appealed, and the appellate court reversed those judgments. (99 Ill. App.3d 271, 54 Ill.Dec. 751, 425 N.E.2d 968.) We granted the defendants leave to appeal under Rule 315 (73 Ill.2d R. 315).

Both suits were filed in the circuit court of Cook County. *Cockrum v. Baumgartner* was brought by Donna and Leon Cockrum against Dr. George Baumgartner and a laboratory that performed tests according to Dr. Baumgartner's instructions. The Cockrums alleged that Dr. Baumgartner negligently performed a vasectomy upon Leon Cockrum. Also, they claimed that he was negligent in telling them that a sperm test conducted by the laboratory showed no live sperm when he should have known that the laboratory report showed that the vasectomy had been medically unsuccessful. The Cockrums also alleged that after the attempted vasectomy Donna Cockrum became pregnant and gave birth to a child, and they claimed that she would not have become pregnant if the physician had not been negligent.

ILLUSTRATION #5

Shepard's Illinois Citations

Vol. 447 **NORTHEASTERN REPORTER, 2d SERIES (Illinois Cases)**

592NE[9]140
593NE[8]591
593NE[9]979
594NE[8]262
594NE1267
601NE[2]921
603NE601
Cir. 7
785FS[7]775
14AR3723s
39AR31000s
30AR4422n

—307—

Des Plaines v Industrial Commission 1983

(95Il2d83)
(69IlD90)
522NE[2]108
523NE[3]592
567NE[2]665
575NE[2]1236
10COA1§ 26

—310—

Doyle v Industrial Commission 1983

(95Il2d103)
(69IlD93)
496NE[1]518

—315—

Illinois Central Gulf Railroad Co. v Department of Local Government Affairs 1983

(95Il2d111)
(69IlD98)
s 428NE557
507NE[9]493
507NE1334
508NE472
510NE567
513NE589
517NE1183
517NE1202
545NE786
570NE525
571NE992
590NE481
604NE1005

—330—

Illinois v Creek 1983

(94Il2d526)
(69IlD113)
s 414NE816
s 429NE1199
469NE[4]584
470NE[2]1127
526NE[4]1384
539NE462
546NE[4]1090
599NE[3]496
599NE[4]496
9AR3203s

—334—

Couri v Couri 1983

(95Il2d91)
(69IlD117)
s 431NE711
497NE1226
501NE190
516NE[8]726
529NE[2]999
529NE[3]999
545NE[1]308
545NE[2]310
565NE[1]152
573NE[1]1288
582NE[2]205
582NE[3]205
605NE[1]651
Cir. 7
691FS[1]73
707FS[1]996
708FS[1]1495

—339—

Interlake Inc. v Industrial Commission 1983

(95Il2d181)
(69IlD122)
475NE[5]233
h 481NE[4]1281
h 481NE[5]1281
488NE[5]648
489NE[5]464
489NE[6]464
492NE[5]1353
494NE[5]1264
499NE[6]1313
500NE[5]956
500NE[6]956
502NE[5]1045
d 504NE[4]85
j 504NE87
j 504NE88
509NE[5]1018
518NE[6]448
521NE[5]295
535NE[5]802

—345—

Waukegan Community Unit School District No. 60 v Waukegan 1983

(95Il2d244)
(69IlD128)
450NE1195
h 457NE[1]1022
e 458NE[2]3
f 467NE[4]1105
d 473NE[2]945
478NE447
478NE[1]448
d 494NE[1]607
j 508NE753
528NE982
540NE[1]977

—353—

Illinois v Davis 1983

(95Il2d1)
(69IlD136)
US reh den
in 465US1014
in 104SC1017
r 449NE815
s 464US1001
s 78LE697
s 104SC507
cc 452NE525
cc 518NE78
449NE[2]554
f 449NE[1]556
j 449NE816
450NE[1]1327
f 452NE108
e 452NE109
453NE[2]1320
f 453NE[2]1325
453NE[2]1327
454NE225
e 454NE[2]230
j 454NE287
454NE[1]333
454NE[2]333
f 456NE[2]1377
456NE[23]1377
457NE[1]1203
j 457NE1210
f 459NE[2]1141
f 459NE[3]1141
461NE[40]357
461NE[31]358
461NE[35]421
j 463NE729
464NE[25]269
f 464NE[31]270
464NE[23]1089
464NE[23]1194
f 468NE1216
f 468NE[45]1218
j 468NE1228
468NE[3]1240
469NE[1]598
469NE[2]598
470NE[29]1203
471NE[18]978
473NE[18]357
473NE[23]862
473NE[31]865
f 473NE866
473NE[2]890
473NE[3]890
f 473NE893
473NE1235
473NE[40]1242
473NE[6]1254
473NE1265
475NE[28]850
475NE[2]1003
478NE[2]298
f 478NE[41]310
c 478NE311
478NE396
478NE[23]1345
480NE[1]1301
481NE[23]676
481NE[23]697
483NE258
483NE612
483NE[19]1342
e 488NE[38]539
489NE[18]853
j 489NE1339
491NE[23]72
492NE[3]910
494NE[40]481
f 495NE[29]1382
496NE[29]1228
497NE[29]149
499NE1348
501NE[19]212
503NE265
f 503NE[31]269
503NE[32]272
504NE[1]842
504NE[2]842
504NE[3]842
509NE[2]485
510NE[29]111
513NE[29]533
516NE450
518NE[40]94
f 518NE98
f 518NE115
518NE[2]773
525NE[43]46
533NE[29]1169
d 535NE904
d 535NE[31]905
538NE[40]475
538NE478
538NE495
538NE[3]1109
539NE[40]1207
j 539NE1214
539NE1320
541NE[29]160
d 541NE[5]196
542NE[8]67
f 542NE[28]918
f 542NE[29]918
542NE[5]1197
e 544NE[31]325
544NE[27]375
547NE[19]154
552NE[30]757
558NE[23]186
f 560NE[29]1235
561NE[29]1198
563NE[8]1191
565NE[17]943
568NE849
569NE[29]330
569NE[28]331
579NE365
e 586NE[33]683
592NE[29]7
f 593NE[29]538
598NE977
603NE[29]1279
f 604NE[31]285
j 604NE293
604NE[8]307
604NE[15]422
d 608NE264
481US[45]155
j 481US174
95LE[45]142
j 95LE155
107SC[45]1686
j 107SC1697
55USLW4501
j 55USLW4506
Cir. 7
j 820F2d850
Cir. 8
715F2d[3]1318
JuS(2)§ 8.12
1AR31291s
67AR3245s
65AR4759n
65AR4879n

—385—

Cockrum v Baumgartner 1983

(95Il2d193)
(69IlD168)
US cert den
in 464US846
in 104SC149
s 425NE968
451NE17
451NE1260
468NE[2]1234
471NE533
d 471NE[1]536
d 471NE[2]536
j 473NE404
d 480NE[1]1229
499NE[1]76
499NE[2]77
499NE[2]407
509NE168
d 512NE[2]703
j 512NE708
e 529NE213
c 529NE[1]218
557NE307
562NE265
Cir. 11
795FS1123
9MeLR210
11MeLR114
13MeLR140
3COA83§ 3
83AR315s
69AR4884n
89AR4642n

—394—

Kozak v Retirement Board of the Firemen's Annuity and Benefit Fund of Chicago 1983

(95Il2d211)
(69IlD177)
s 425NE1371
s 470NE1293
j 449NE86
452NE[1]762
452NE[1]767
456NE[7]136
468NE[5]1273
474NE763
481NE[4]728
481NE[1]1288
482NE[7]1084
e 483NE12
485NE[3]522
485NE[1]1079
485NE[4]1079
485NE[5]1079
487NE[1]1008
f 488NE[3]1055
f 488NE[7]1363
492NE[4]238
494NE[1]642
494NE[1]1264
f 496NE[1]254
f 496NE[3]254
f 496NE[4]254
499NE[3]986
503NE[7]821
504NE[4]810
506NE[4]671
509NE[7]168
510NE[1]1189
510NE1225
j 514NE259

APPENDIX D

Sample Memorandum:
Bell-Wesley v. O'Toole

MEMORANDUM

TO: Jane Harvey

FROM: Heather Joseph

RE: <u>Bell-Wesley v. O'Toole</u>:
           Damages for wrongful pregnancy

DATE: August 28, 1995

I.
Question Presented

Can the parents of a healthy, normal child, born subsequent to a negligently performed sterilization operation, recover the cost of raising the child in a wrongful pregnancy action?

II.
Brief Answer

Yes. However, child-rearing damages are unlikely in the <u>Bell-Wesley</u> case. This issue is one of first impression in Ames; other jurisdictions are divided. A majority of jurisdictions do not allow any recovery for child-rearing costs. Five jurisdictions require that such a recovery be offset by the benefit the parents will receive from the child in the form of aid and affection (the "benefit rule"). Two jurisdictions provide for full recovery of the costs of raising a child to majority.

III.
Statement of Facts

Rebecca and Scott Bell-Wesley made a conscious decision to forego having children after Rebecca had

136

three successive pregnancies, which resulted in congenitally deformed children, each of whom died in infancy. (R.1) Dr. Stephen O'Toole, the Bell-Wesleys' physician, informed them that there was a seventy-five percent probability that any child they conceived would suffer the same congenital deformity. (R.1) With this information, the Bell-Wesleys chose to remain childless. Although they could have adopted, they decided to devote their time and energy to their careers and to each other. (R.1) Their decision to forego children was for therapeutic reasons (their desire to avoid having another congenitally deformed child), rather than for economic reasons. (R.11) On October 16, 1993, Dr. O'Toole performed a vasectomy on Scott Bell-Wesley to insure that the couple would not conceive any more children. (R.1) Three months later, Dr. O'Toole performed a sperm count on Scott Bell-Wesley and informed the Bell-Wesleys that the operation had been successful. (R.2) The Bell-Wesleys resumed marital relations with the belief that Scott was sterile. (R.2)

In April 1995, Rebecca discovered that she was pregnant. (R.2) The Bell-Wesleys decided not to abort the child on moral grounds, and they also chose to forego an amniocentesis. (R.8,12) The couple experienced a great deal of anxiety during the pregnancy given their prior experiences and their decision not to have children. (R.3) Rebecca gave birth to a healthy baby boy, Frank Michael Bell, on January 4, 1996. (R.2) The Bell-Wesleys decided to keep the child and not put him up for adoption. (R.12)

2

The trial court concluded as a matter of law that Dr. O'Toole's negligence was the proximate cause of this pregnancy. He not only failed to sever Scott's vas deferens properly, but he also negligently performed Scott's sperm count in January 1994. (R.12)

Rebecca's unexpected pregnancy and the subsequent birth of Frank have resulted in injury to the Bell-Wesleys. They were forced to pay substantial medical bills in connection with the pregnancy and delivery of the baby. (R.3) Rebecca underwent significant pain and suffering as a result of the unexpected pregnancy and birth. (R.3) Both parties also underwent substantial mental trauma throughout the pregnancy and birth of a child whom they expected to be deformed. They seek compensation for loss of consortium and lost wages. (R.3) Finally, the Bell-Wesleys allege that they are now faced with a substantial unexpected and unwanted financial burden -- the cost of raising a child to his majority. (R.3)

The Bell-Wesleys filed a wrongful pregnancy suit against Dr. Stephen O'Toole to force him to pay all of the foreseeable costs of the negligent medical care he provided to Scott. (R.1-4) The Superior Court recognized that Dr. O'Toole had been negligent and that this was the proximate cause of the unexpected pregnancy. (R.12) The Superior Court awarded the Bell-Wesleys damages for the medical costs incident to the pregnancy and birth of the child, as well as pain and suffering, and loss of consortium, but refused to award damages for the cost of raising the child. (R.13-14) The Bell-Wesleys appealed the trial court's ruling on child-rearing costs to the Court of Appeals for the State of Ames (N.E. Division), which affirmed the trial court's decision. (R.18) This case is now on appeal to the Supreme Court of Ames.

3

IV.
Discussion

A. <u>Introduction</u>

   The Bell-Wesleys have a cause of action in tort for either wrongful conception or wrongful pregnancy (the terms are interchangeable -- hereinafter "wrongful pregnancy"). A wrongful pregnancy cause of action arises when parents take medical steps which fail to prevent pregnancy and result in the birth of a healthy child. In some jurisdictions this claim is properly pursued as a simple negligence claim; in others it is a distinct tort. This cause of action should be distinguished from two similar prenatal common law tort actions: (1) a wrongful birth cause of action (suit by parents claiming they would have avoided conception or terminated the pregnancy if they had been properly advised of the risks or existence of birth defects in the potential child); and (2) an action for wrongful life (action brought by an impaired child, in which it is alleged that but for the defendant's negligent treatment or advice, the child would not have been born). <u>See</u> Russell G. Donaldson, Annotation, <u>Recoverability of Cost of Raising Normal, Healthy Child Born as Result of Physician's Negligence or Breach of Warranty</u>, 89 A.L.R.4th 632 (1994) (describing the three prenatal causes of action).

B. <u>Child-Rearing Costs as an Element of Wrongful Pregnancy Damages</u>

   The Bell-Wesleys' recovery of child-rearing costs depends upon the damages rule adopted by the Supreme Court of Ames. Courts have taken four approaches to the

4

award of damages in wrongful pregnancy causes of action:
(1) no recovery at all; (2) limited recovery (allows
recovery for consequential damages until termination of
the pregnancy, but no recovery for child-rearing costs);
(3) the benefit rule (permits consequential damages plus
recovery for child-rearing costs offset by the value of
aid and comfort given to parents by the child); and (4)
full recovery for all costs flowing from the wrongful
pregnancy.

The approach embraced by any given jurisdiction turns
on the weight accorded various policy considerations.
There is no clear trend in the case law. While most
states have adopted limited damages, two states have
recently become the first states unequivocally to adopt
full damages. At the same time, two of the first states
to adopt the benefit rule have recanted and seem to be
moving back to limited damages. The Bell-Wesleys should
argue for full recovery. Arguing for the benefit rule
may lead to a substantially lower recovery, and the
Supreme Court of Ames may well turn to it as a
compromise between full damages and limited damages.
The following is an analysis of each of the four damages
rules which the Supreme Court of Ames may adopt.

1. <u>No Recovery</u>

The Bell-Wesleys are almost certainly entitled to
some recovery in this action. Of the states which have
addressed wrongful pregnancy, Nevada alone does not
provide for any recovery for this tort claim. In a 1986
case, the Supreme Court of Nevada held that there was no
tort liability in cases of wrongful pregnancy because an
essential element of a negligence tort was lacking:
damages. That court felt that the birth of a healthy

5

child was simply not a "legally compensable injurious consequence." See Szekeres v. Robinson, 715 P.2d 1076, 1077 (Nev. 1986) (family sued for damages following failed sterilization procedure on mother). However, the Szekeres court did allow the case to proceed as a breach of contract claim. Id. at 1078. While the Supreme Court of Ames could conceivably accept the rationale of the Nevada court that the birth of a healthy baby does not in any way constitute a compensable injury, such a ruling would conflict with the overwhelming majority of precedent on this issue.

2. Limited Damages

The Supreme Court of Ames may well affirm the lower courts' adoption of the limited damages rule in the Bell-Wesley case. A majority of jurisdictions (twenty-seven) has limited the damages the parents may recover in a wrongful pregnancy suit to damages resulting from the pregnancy and birth, but excluding the costs of raising the child.[1] The rationales for so limiting the damages vary, but most justifications are anchored in the notion that the birth of a normal, healthy child constitutes a net benefit to the parents, not a compensable harm. Other rationales include: concern over the psyche of the child; the speculative nature of the damages; concern that awarding damages would provide parents with a windfall and unfairly penalize the physician; and a refusal to award damages

---

[1]Alabama, Arkansas, Delaware, District of Columbia, Florida, Georgia, Illinois, Iowa, Kansas, Kentucky, Louisiana, Maine, Missouri, New Hampshire, New Jersey, New York, North Carolina, Ohio, Oklahoma, Pennsylvania, Tennessee, Texas, Utah, Virginia, Washington, and West Virginia have all adopted the limited damages rule.

6

when the parents chose sterilization for non-economic
reasons (i.e., therapeutic or eugenic reasons related to
the parents' peace of mind).

   (a) *Birth of a Healthy Child is Not a Compensable*
        Injury

   A significant number of courts have refused to award
child-rearing costs on the grounds that the birth of a
healthy child is not an injury, or in the alternative,
that the benefits always outweigh the costs. In either
case, there is no compensable injury. See, e.g.,
Cockrum v. Baumgartner, 447 N.E.2d 385 (Ill. 1983)
(holding that public policy forbids imposition of normal
tort rule that a tortfeasor be liable for all the costs
of his tortious conduct in wrongful pregnancy context);
O'Toole v. Greenberg, 477 N.E.2d 445 (N.Y. 1985)
(holding that in wrongful conception case stemming from
negligently performed, unsuccessful tubal ligation,
plaintiffs could not recover the costs of child-rearing
because as a matter of public policy parents suffered no
legally cognizable harm); Johnson v. Univ. Hosp. of
Cleveland, 540 N.E.2d 1370 (Ohio 1989) (holding that on
public policy grounds birth of a healthy child cannot be
an injury). The Supreme Court of Ames may adopt this
rationale and deny the Bell-Wesleys further damages,
reasoning that they have already been fully compensated
for their injuries relating to wrongful pregnancy.

   (b) *Psychological Injury*

   Some courts refuse to award damages for child-rearing
on the grounds that such awards would adversely affect
the unplanned child's psyche. See, e.g., Wilbur v.
Kerr, 628 S.W.2d 568, 571 (Ark. 1982) ("We are also

convinced that the damage to the child will be significant; that ... some day learn[ing] that its parents did not want it and, in fact, went to court to force someone else to pay for its raising, will be harmful to that child.").

If the Ames Supreme Court finds the injured psyche argument persuasive, it will rule against the Bell-Wesleys on the grounds that Frank might be hurt psychologically when he finds out that a third party is paying in whole or in part for his upbringing, and that he was an unplanned child. This argument fails for two reasons, however. First, many children are unplanned but function well despite knowledge of the circumstances of their conception. Second, taken to its logical conclusion, this argument demands that no damages of any sort be awarded because the child will be injured if it finds out -- yet some damages have already been awarded. While other courts have ignored such inconsistencies, see, e.g., Wilbur, 628 S.W.2d at 571 (permitting award of any and all proper damages connected with the operation and the pregnancy, but not child-rearing costs), a strong argument can be made that Ames should not do so.

   (c) *Too Speculative*

The argument that child-rearing costs are too speculative is similarly unconvincing. Courts can calculate damages in this area much more easily than in a number of other contexts, such as wrongful death, where damages are regularly awarded. Tort cases routinely require the calculation of damages that are much more speculative, such as pain and suffering, emotional distress, and loss of consortium.

8

Nonetheless, a number of courts cite difficulties in calculating damages as justifying their refusal to award child-rearing costs. <u>See, e.g.</u>, <u>Boone v. Mullendoore</u>, 416 So. 2d 718, 722 (Ala. 1982) (rejecting benefit rule as inviting "speculative and ethically questionable assessments of damages"); <u>Hitzemann v. Adam</u>, 518 N.W.2d 102 (Neb. 1994) (noting that only the following could be properly recovered in a wrongful pregnancy suit: prenatal and delivery medical expenses; emotional distress, loss of wages, pain and suffering, and loss of consortium caused by the failed sterilization, pregnancy, and childbirth; and the costs of a second sterilization procedure).

The costs of clothing, feeding and providing for the education of Frank Bell would be more easily calculated than some of the damages already awarded by the trial court in this case (i.e., mental anguish of the parents, loss of consortium). The Court could easily rely on government studies of the economic costs of raising children as a baseline for assessing child-rearing damages. <u>See</u> Exhibit A, (R.5).

   (d) *Windfall*

Some courts have refused to award child-rearing costs as an unjust windfall to parents who are receiving the benefits of the child's companionship. <u>See, e.g.</u>, <u>Berman v. Allan</u>, 404 A.2d 8 (N.J. 1979). Courts espousing the windfall rationale are concerned with the injustice they perceive in enabling parents to enjoy all the benefits of having a child, while bearing none of the costs. Precluding recovery in wrongful pregnancy cases, however, leads to under-deterrence: physicians

9

may not be as careful in performing sterilizations as they would be if they knew they would have to pay for the costs of raising a subsequently conceived child. Moreover, physicians can buy insurance covering the rare occasions when a sterilization procedure fails, so that the financial burden on physicians should not be great. Requiring payment for child-rearing costs is nothing more than enforcing the ordinary tort damage rule that one should pay all of the foreseeable costs of one's tortious behavior.

One possible compromise would be to offset the parents' perceived "windfall" by subtracting the benefits that accrued to the parents -- effectively the benefit rule. Because of the availability of insurance for physicians, the unjust windfall argument rings hollow in the Bell-Wesley case and should not be a bar to the recovery of child-rearing costs.

 (e) *Sterilization Done For Eugenic or Therapeutic*
   Reasons

Some courts have refused to award damages for child-rearing when the sterilization procedure was undertaken not for economic reasons, but for therapeutic (concern for the mother's health) or eugenic (avoidance of a feared genetic defect) ones. In Hartke v. McKelway, 707 F.2d 1544, 1554 (D.C. Cir. 1983), the United States Court of Appeals for the District of Columbia held that the plaintiff could recover damages for medical costs and pain and suffering, but could not do so for child-rearing expenses. The plaintiff had undergone a tubal ligation, not for economic reasons, but out of fear for her life should she become pregnant again after experiencing an ectopic pregnancy. The

10

court reasoned that it was the pregnancy she sought to avoid through sterilization, not the child; therefore she need be compensated for only the nine months of pregnancy. <u>See also</u> <u>Burke v. Rivo</u>, 551 N.E.2d 1, 5-6 (Mass. 1990) (holding that justification for child-rearing damages lessened where eugenic or therapeutic reasons motivated the desire to avoid birth of a child). In the present case, this reasoning would lead to a decision not to allow damages for child-rearing costs to the Bell-Wesleys. The Bell-Wesleys are not under financial strain, and the primary reason for Scott's sterilization appears to be eugenic. Once a healthy baby was born, the Bell-Wesleys were happy to have him. It is not at all clear that any injury to the Bell-Wesleys extends to the post-conception period.

In response, the Bell-Wesleys could argue that even though the couple wanted a child before the vasectomy, they had changed their minds, and the unplanned birth of Frank was an imposition on their constitutionally protected right to control procreation. Several facts support this argument: the Bell-Wesleys chose not to adopt; they had resigned themselves to a childless life; and Mrs. Bell-Wesley accepted a new position with the state Attorney General's office in reliance upon their decision not to have children. Nonetheless, the Bell-Wesleys are likely to be denied child-rearing damages because the facts indicate that they underwent the vasectomy for non-economic reasons. Once a healthy baby was born free of the congenital deformities associated with their earlier pregnancies, they were not entitled to any further compensation.

11

3. <u>Benefit Rule</u>

If the Supreme Court of Ames chooses to adopt the benefit rule, the Bell-Wesleys will recover some, but not all, of their child-rearing costs. A number of jurisdictions has adopted the benefit rule in the wrongful pregnancy context. It is the rule in five states (Arizona, California, Connecticut, Maryland, and Massachusetts) and was the rule in two others where its status is now uncertain (Michigan and Minnesota). The benefit rule usually allows recovery of child-rearing expenses until the child reaches majority, but these expenses must be offset by the benefit the parents will receive in aid and comfort from the child. The benefit rule was drawn from section 920 of the Restatement (Second) of Torts. Section 920 states that

> [w]hen the defendant's tortious conduct has caused harm to the plaintiff or to his property and in doing so has conferred a special benefit to the interest of the plaintiff that was harmed, the value of the benefit conferred is considered in mitigation of damages, to the extent that it is equitable.

Restatement (Second) of Torts § 920 (1972).

There are two main criticisms of the benefit rule. First, the benefit provided by the child is very difficult to quantify. Second, contradicting the Restatement, the interest benefited is not the same as the one harmed. While the birth of a healthy child may confer some benefits on the parents, these benefits involve interests distinct from those harmed by the health care provider's negligence. The emotional benefits received by the parents are of an entirely different nature than the financial injuries imposed upon the parents. See <u>Johnson v. Univ. Hosp. of Cleveland</u>, 540 N.E.2d 1370 (Ohio 1989) (holding that

12

benefit rule fails to comply with the Restatement
because it requires jury to weigh pecuniary costs
against non-pecuniary benefits).

Supporters of the benefit rule contend that the
calculation for aid and comfort is the same calculation
done in the wrongful death context and should be no more
difficult. The benefit rule is an effort to exert
optimal deterrence on health care providers while
keeping the parents from receiving a windfall.

The first court to apply the benefit rule in a
wrongful pregnancy action was a Michigan appellate court
in Troppi v. Scarf, 187 N.W.2d 511 (Mich. Ct. App.
1971). In that case, the plaintiff, a mother of seven,
brought suit against a pharmacist who had negligently
filled her birth control prescription with
tranquilizers, thus allowing her to become pregnant with
her eighth child. Id. The Michigan court was willing
to permit recovery for the costs of rearing the child
until majority, but held that this award should be
reduced by the amount of benefit conferred upon the
plaintiff by the child's birth. The Troppi court based
its decision on section 920 of the Restatement of Torts.
While Michigan was the progenitor of the benefit rule, a
1989 decision by a Michigan appellate court endorsed the
limited damages rule, and the status of the benefit rule
in Michigan is currently unclear. See Rinard v. Biczak,
441 N.W.2d 441 (Mich. Ct. App. 1989) (holding in a
failure to diagnose pregnancy case that costs of raising
normal, healthy child not recoverable).

The status of the benefit rule is also unclear in
Minnesota. In Sherlock v. Stillwater Clinic, 260 N.W.2d
169 (Minn. 1977), a failed vasectomy case, the Minnesota

13

Supreme Court held that the benefit rule was the correct way to measure child-rearing damages. However, dicta in a more recent Minnesota Supreme Court decision has cast some doubt on that ruling without expressly overruling it. See Hickman v. Group Health Plan, Inc., 396 N.W.2d 10 (Minn. 1986) (suggesting that Sherlock decision may have been erroneous). Both Michigan and Minnesota, among the first jurisdictions to adopt the benefit rule, are now backing away from it toward limited damages.

In 1990, the Supreme Judicial Court of Massachusetts held that parents in the wrongful pregnancy context could recover child-rearing costs offset by any benefit, if they had sought the sterilization for economic reasons. Burke v. Rivo, 551 N.E.2d 1, 6 (Mass. 1990). The Burke court endorsed the position that the justification for awarding child-rearing costs was far less compelling when the parents sought sterilization for eugenic or therapeutic reasons. Id. While the Burke court did not explicitly preclude recovery for child-rearing costs when the primary motivation for sterilization was not economic, it seemed to frown on a damage award under such circumstances. Id. at 5-6.

The Supreme Judicial Court of Massachusetts noted that many of the justifications used by courts that refused to award child-rearing damages in the wrongful pregnancy context were unimpressive. In particular, the Supreme Judicial Court found the conclusion that the benefits of having the child always outweighed the economic loss lacked "verisimilitude." Id. at 4. The Burke court felt that the very fact that a person sought medical intervention to prevent a pregnancy was proof enough for such person that the benefits of parenthood did not outweigh the burdens of having a child. Id.

14

The _Burke_ court rejected the argument that child-rearing damages should not be awarded because the child's psyche could be injured when it found out it had been unwanted and someone else had paid to help raise it. As noted by the Supreme Judicial Court, such a position demanded that no damages be awarded. Yet courts which cited this rationale allowed damages to be awarded for other expenses incident to the unwanted pregnancy. _Id._ at 4-5.

The court rejected the first major criticism of the benefit rule -- the difficulty of determining the value of the child to its parents. The court aptly noted that state law recognized the propriety of measuring the loss to parents in financial terms when a child is seriously injured or killed, and that to measure the benefit is simply the reverse side of the coin. The court noted but did not address the second major criticism of the benefit rule, that an offset was inappropriate under section 920. The Bell-Wesleys' claim for child-rearing costs is weak under the analysis of the _Burke_ court because Scott's sterilization was done not for economic reasons but for eugenic and therapeutic reasons. However, even the _Burke_ court did not reject child-rearing damages outright in the absence of economic imperatives.

Courts in five states have adopted the benefit rule; its status in two others, Minnesota and Michigan, is uncertain. For other jurisdictions which have adopted the benefit rule, see _University of Arizona Health Sciences Ctr. v. Superior Court of County of Maricopa_, 667 P.2d 1294 (Ariz. 1983);

15

<u>Morris v. Frudenfeld</u>, 185 Cal. Rptr. 76 (Cal. Ct. App.
1982); <u>Stills v. Gratton</u>, 127 Cal. Rptr. 652 (Cal. Ct.
App. 1976); <u>Ochs v. Borrelli</u>, 445 A.2d 883 (Conn. 1982);
<u>Jones v. Malinowski</u>, 473 A.2d 429 (Md. 1984) (rejecting
view that birth of a healthy baby should as a matter of
law always outweigh the expense of raising it and
holding that jury serves as a check on unwarranted
damage awards).

    4. <u>Full Recovery</u>

    The Bell-Wesleys can recover all the costs of raising
their unplanned child only if the Supreme Court of Ames
adopts the full recovery rule. States allowing for full
recovery in wrongful pregnancy suits demand that the
tortfeasor bear the foreseeable costs of his or her
tortious conduct, including the costs of raising a
normal, healthy child to majority. Full recovery is
currently the rule in two states, Wisconsin and New
Mexico. <u>See</u> <u>Lovelace Medical Ctr. v. Mendez</u>, 805 P.2d
603 (N.M. 1991); <u>Marciniak v. Lundborg</u>, 450 N.W.2d 243
(Wis. 1990) (rejecting benefit rule because when
properly applied, section 920 of Restatement (Second) of
Torts does not provide an offset in this context).

    The first case to suggest that child-rearing costs
were appropriate in a cause of action for wrongful
pregnancy was <u>Custodio v. Bauer</u>, 59 Cal. Rptr. 463 (Cal.
Ct. App. 1967). However, other California courts have
not followed this decision and have held that the
benefit rule is the proper rule in California for
damages in wrongful pregnancy. <u>See</u> <u>Morris v.
Frudenfeld</u>, 185 Cal. Rptr. 76 (Cal. Ct. App. 1982);
<u>Stills v. Gratton</u>, 127 Cal. Rptr. 652 (Cal. Ct. App.
1976).

                              16

In <u>Lovelace Medical Center v. Mendez</u>, 805 P.2d 603 (N.M. 1991), the Supreme Court of New Mexico held that the parents of a normal, healthy baby conceived as the result of a negligently performed, unsuccessful sterilization operation could recover the costs of raising the child from birth to adulthood. The court rejected the claim that the birth of a healthy child cannot be an injury. The court stated that the harm was not the birth of the child, but the invasion of the parents' legally protected interest in the financial security of their family and the frustration of their desire to limit the size of their family. <u>Id.</u> at 612-13. The reasoning of the <u>Mendez</u> court does not strongly support the Bell-Wesleys, because they did not seek sterilization for financial reasons. Rather, they did so out of concern that any child born to them would have a seventy-five percent chance of suffering the same congenital defect which led to the premature death of their previous children. The primary "harm" to the Bell-Wesleys was the emotional trauma they experienced during the pregnancy as they anticipated that they would give birth to another deformed child. While the Bell-Wesleys should be fully compensated for their emotional trauma during the pregnancy, they may not be entitled to the cost of raising their healthy child under <u>Lovelace</u>.

However, the Bell-Wesleys may argue that they are entitled to full recovery nonetheless, because the failed sterilization resulted in an invasion of the Bell-Wesleys' constitutionally protected right to control the size of their family. <u>See</u> <u>Roe v. Wade</u>, 410 U.S. 113 (1973) (affirming that the Constitution guarantees the right to privacy); <u>Griswold v.</u>

17

<u>Connecticut</u>, 381 U.S. 479 (1965) (recognizing a
constitutionally protected zone of privacy in which
couples make family planning decisions). The
Bell-Wesleys made a decision to forego children and
decided not to adopt. Because a child was forced upon
them against their will through the doctor's negligence,
they should be compensated.

Full recovery would be the most advantageous damage
rule for the Bell-Wesleys; however, a ruling for full
damages by the Ames Supreme Court in this case is
unlikely. Full recovery has been adopted by only two
states, and the persuasive value of <u>Mendez</u> is lessened
in this case, because the unplanned birth of Frank did
not threaten the family's financial security.

C. <u>Standard of Review</u>

The standard of review on the proper rule of damages
in a wrongful pregnancy action is de novo. <u>See</u> <u>Sherlock
v. Stillwater Clinic</u>, 260 N.W.2d 169, 172 (Minn. 1977)
(noting that decisions of law are reviewed de novo).

V.
Conclusion

While it is possible that the Bell-Wesleys will be
awarded child-rearing damages, such a result is unlikely
given the weight of case law and the importance of
non-economic reasons for the sterilization. The
Bell-Wesleys' recovery of child-rearing costs in the
wrongful pregnancy context largely depends upon the
Supreme Court of Ames's view on two questions: (1)
whether public policy concerns demand that normal tort
damage rules be set aside in the wrongful pregnancy
context because the "injury" is a healthy, human child;

18

and (2) if so, under the benefit analysis the extent
to which this economic injury to the parents is
outweighed by the benefits of having a healthy child.
Traditional tort rules indicate that the tortfeasor
should bear all of the costs of his wrongful conduct, or
under-deterrence will result. The opposing side in this
context, however, has a strong emotional argument that
wrongful pregnancy is a special situation because human
life is involved, and substantial intangible benefits
have accrued to the parents through the birth of the
healthy child. In sum, it is unlikely that the
Bell-Wesleys will be awarded child-rearing costs.

VI.
Scope of Research

A search of the A.L.R. Index and Quick Index under
"vasectomy" and "wrongful birth" led to several
annotations, including a recent one on child-rearing
damages for wrongful pregnancy. Russell G. Donaldson,
Annotation, Recoverability of Cost of Raising Normal,
Healthy Child Born As Result of Physician's Negligence
or Breach of Contract or Warranty, 89 A.L.R. 4th 632
(1994). The search "'wrongful conception' or 'wrongful
pregnancy'" in WESTLAW's LRI database uncovered several
recent articles on wrongful pregnancy actions. See
David J. Burke, Wrongful Pregnancy: Child Rearing
Damages Deserve Full Judicial Consideration, 8 Pace L.
Rev. 313 (1988); Judy S. Lotherstein, Toward Full
Recovery--The Future of Damage Awards in Wrongful
Pregnancy Cases, 25 Suffolk U. L. Rev. 735 (1991).

19

The articles and annotation included a number of case
citations, which I updated with the following searches:

> FAMILY library/OMNI file in LEXIS: wrongful birth or
> wrongful pregnancy and vasectomy or sterilization.

> MFL-CS (multistate cases on family law) in WESTLAW:
> "wrongful conception" or "wrongful pregnancy" or "wrong-
> ful birth" and vasectomy or sterilization.

Also on WESTLAW, I searched "'wrongful pregnancy' or
'wrongful birth' and 299k18.110" to use the West topic
and key number for "Physicians and Surgeons: Damages."

To ensure that the cases were current, I Shepardized
all of the cases cited above. I also ran a search in
WESTLAW's STAT-ALL to check for state statutes
regulating these causes of action with the search:
"'wrongful birth' or 'wrongful pregnancy' or 'wrongful
conception.'"

20

APPENDIX E

Sample Briefs:
Bell-Wesley v. O'Toole

IN THE SUPREME COURT OF THE

STATE OF AMES

CIVIL ACTION NO. 96-2004

SCOTT AND REBECCA BELL-WESLEY, PLAINTIFFS-APPELLANTS

V.

DR.STEPHEN O'TOOLE, DEFENDANT-APPELLEE

BRIEF FOR THE PLAINTIFFS-APPELLANTS

Jane E. Harvey
Attorney for the
Plaintiffs-Appellants

Argument: December 14, 1996
Ames Courtroom
7:30 p.m.

TABLE OF CONTENTS

TABLE OF AUTHORITIES

CASES

ii

159

QUESTIONS PRESENTED

Should a doctor whose negligent performance of sterilization procedures led to the birth of an unwanted
child be held liable for the full extent of his negligence, including the extensive financial costs associated with the birth and upbringing of the child?

If the court will not award full damages, should a
family who has been traumatized financially and emotion-
ally by a negligently performed sterilization be denied
any recovery merely because of the reason they obtained
the sterilization?

INTRODUCTION

Fundamental tort goals of deterrence and fairness require Dr. O'Toole to pay for the reasonably foreseeable
consequences of his failure to perform properly Scott
Bell-Wesley's vasectomy and subsequent sperm count.
Once two people have exercised their constitutional
right to determine that their family will be childless,
any violation of that right must be redressed. The fact
that Frank Michael Bell is a healthy, normal child
should not prevent his parents from recovering the costs
they had consciously chosen to avoid. To hold otherwise
would be to excuse doctors for their negligent care, on
the basis that some consequences of their negligence are
positive, regardless of whether the individual patients
agree. The fact that Frank is a baby should be immate-
rial to this Court's decision; Dr. O'Toole is not God.
This Court should award the Bell-Wesleys the costs of

1

raising Frank to majority, rather than allowing Dr.
O'Toole to force the Bell-Wesleys to live a life he
designed without recompense.

STATEMENT OF THE CASE

Rebecca and Scott Bell-Wesley made a conscious decision to forego having children. (R.1) Three of their
children died in infancy due to congenital defects.
(R.1) Their doctor, Dr. Stephen O'Toole, informed them
that there was a seventy-five percent probability that
any child they conceived would suffer from the same congenital deformity. Given their previous failures, the
information from their doctor, and a fear of bringing a
deformed child into the world, Rebecca and Scott Bell-
Wesley chose to remain childless. (R.1,11) They did not
adopt. Instead, they elected to devote their lives to
each other and to their occupations. Scott is an architect with the Holmes City Planning Department, and
Rebecca is an attorney with the Attorney Generals Office
of the State of Ames. (R.1,9) In order to ensure the
childless lifestyle they had chosen, Rebecca and Scott
had Dr. O'Toole perform a vasectomy on Scott on October
16, 1993. (R.1) Dr. O'Toole subsequently checked
Scott's sperm count and informed the Bell-Wesleys that
the operation had been a success -- Scott was sterile.
(R.2)

Based on the choices she and Scott had made about
their lifestyle, Rebecca accepted a position as First Assistant Attorney General of the State of Ames in 1993,
shortly after her husband's vasectomy. (R.9) Rebecca
and Scott also resumed marital relations after Dr.
O'Toole informed them that the operation had been a
success.

2

In April 1995, Rebecca Bell-Wesley discovered that
she was pregnant. Even though Rebecca and Scott feared
their child would be deformed like the previous three,
they decided against abortion on moral grounds. (R.12)
They also chose not to undergo amniocentesis. (R.8) On
January 4, 1996, Rebecca Bell-Wesley gave birth to a
healthy baby boy, Frank Michael. (R.2) The Superior
Court concluded that Dr. O'Toole's negligence caused
this birth. (R.12) Dr. O'Toole failed to sever the
tubes of Scott's vas deferens properly. (R.11) Dr.
O'Toole compounded his negligence by misperforming the
sperm count which led the Bell-Wesleys to believe the initial operation had been performed properly. (R.11)

The Bell-Wesleys brought this medical malpractice action to recover for the substantial injuries caused by
Dr. O'Toole's carelessness. While Rebecca and Scott
love Frank deeply, his conception and birth have nonetheless caused them severe emotional, physical, and financial harm. In addition to the pain and the substantial
medical expenses related to the pregnancy, the Bell-
Wesleys suffered considerable trauma from the conception
and birth of a child whom they expected to be deformed.
(R.1,3) Frank's birth has forced the Bell-Wesleys to al-
ter their lives dramatically. (R.12) Both parents have
lost, and will continue to lose, time and wages from
their careers in order to care for the child. (R.12) After deciding to remain childless, Rebecca determined to
devote more time to her career and accepted an important
promotion with the Attorney General's office. Her salary increased from $48,000 to $64,000 per year. (R.10)
Rebecca's leave of absence in connection with the pregnancy has placed her job in jeopardy. (R.8) The

3

financial and emotional costs of raising Frank present the Bell-Wesleys with a formidable burden.

The Superior Court recognized Dr. O'Toole's repeated acts of negligence, but limited the recovery to $100,000, covering only the medical costs, pain and suffering, and loss of consortium immediately associated with the vasectomy. (R.12) The Bell-Wesleys appealed to the Court of Appeals for the State of Ames, which affirmed the trial court. (R.15) This Court granted certiorari to determine whether the Bell-Wesleys can recover the costs of raising Frank to majority. (R.17)

ARGUMENT

I. BASIC TORT PRINCIPLES REQUIRE DR. O'TOOLE TO COMPENSATE FULLY THE BELL-WESLEYS FOR ALL FORESEEABLE DAMAGES RESULTING FROM HIS NEGLIGENT STERILIZATION, INCLUDING THE COSTS OF HAVING AND RAISING THEIR CHILD.

Rebecca and Scott Bell-Wesley have sustained serious physical, financial, and emotional injuries as a result of Dr. O'Toole's negligent sterilization and sperm count and are entitled to full recovery for all foreseeable damages. These foreseeable damages include the costs of having and raising their unwanted child. The trial court's denial of the Bell-Wesleys' prayer for compensation for the expense of raising the unwanted child is a finding of law that can and should be overturned. See Sherlock v. Stillwater Clinic, 260 N.W.2d 169, 172 (Minn. 1977) (noting that decisions of law are reviewed de novo).

The standard formula for tort remedies applies to this wrongful pregnancy claim as it does to any medical malpractice action: Dr. O'Toole should be held liable

4

for all injuries flowing naturally and foreseeably from
his repeated negligence. See W. Page Keeton et al.,
Prosser and Keeton on the Law of Torts 43 (5th ed.
1984) (describing theories of liability for negligence).
The obvious consequences of a negligently performed sterilization are the conception and birth of an unplanned
child and the associated costs of pregnancy, birth, and
upbringing. See Custodio v. Bauer, 59 Cal. Rptr. 463,
476 (Cal. Ct. App. 1967) (noting that damages recoverable on remand included the cost of the unsuccessful
operation; mental, physical, and nervous pain and suffering during pregnancy; and costs of rearing the child).

Rebecca and Scott Bell-Wesley should recover for each
of the injuries that O'Toole inflicted upon them,
because the fundamental aim of tort recovery is to place
the victims in the same position they would have been in
had the tort never occurred. The Superior Court's failure to award damages for child-raising has left the
couple uncompensated for significant emotional and
economic harms. The medical expenses associated with
Rebecca's pregnancy and Frank's birth are costs that the
Bell-Wesleys would not have incurred but for O'Toole's
malfeasance. Moreover, Rebecca endured great physical
pain, and both Scott and Rebecca suffered loss of consortium in connection with the pregnancy, injuries for
which they are entitled to further damages. See
Sherlock, 260 N.W.2d at 175 (establishing that prenatal
and postnatal medical expenses, pain and suffering, and
loss of consortium are all damages immediately incident
to pregnancy and birth and should be allowed under ele-
mentary tort principles). The Bell-Wesleys' situation

5

does not warrant any change from standard tort law, because full compensation is necessary to deter negligence
and to insure a proper standard of medical care.

Rebecca and Scott Bell-Wesley are entitled to recover
for all of the injuries resulting from Dr. O'Toole's
defective sterilization operation and sperm count, including their pain and suffering, emotional trauma, lost
earnings, the costs of raising Frank, and the sacrifice
of their chosen lifestyle.

The Bell-Wesleys suffered acute mental anguish after
learning that Rebecca was pregnant. Scott and Rebecca
had experienced three other pregnancies, each resulting
in deformed children who died shortly after birth.
O'Toole had informed them that any future pregnancy was
seventy-five percent likely to have similarly tragic
results. (R.1) Thus, for over eight months, the Bell-
Wesleys lived in fear that Rebecca would give birth to
another deformed child. Their damage award should
reflect the mental suffering O'Toole's negligence inflicted. See Ochs v. Borrelli, 445 A.2d 883, 886
(Conn. 1982) (recognizing that fear of the birth of a
handicapped child is a compensable injury); Hartke v.
McKelway, 707 F.2d 1544, 1555 (D.C. Cir. 1983) (holding
that mother's anxiety about unborn child's potential
deformity merited damage award), cert. denied, 464 U.S.
983 (1983).

Both Scott and Rebecca have lost and will continue to
lose valuable time and earnings in their chosen careers.
Rebecca's leave of absence from her position as
Assistant Attorney General has deprived her of valuable

6

career experience necessary to her professional development and may have jeopardized her job. (R.9) As the
Superior Court noted, Dr. O'Toole's negligence has pro-
foundly altered the Bell-Wesleys' lifestyle. (R.12)
Frank's birth and the resulting responsibilities have
greatly curtailed the financial and emotional freedom
the couple enjoyed. The Bell-Wesleys should be compensated for this economic and emotional strain. See
Custodio, 59 Cal. Rptr. at 476-77 (finding that the
economic and emotional strain that may be associated
with an unexpected pregnancy resulting from negligent
sterilization should be compensated, even when mother
and child survive without complications).

O'Toole's tortious conduct has thrust the extensive
financial burden of raising a child upon Scott and Rebecca. They seek to recover not for Frank's life, but
for the diminution in family wealth that necessarily resulted from his birth. See Custodio, 59 Cal. Rptr. at
477 (providing that in negligent sterilization case, recovery of economic damages is available to place the family in the same economic position in which it would have
been without the unintended birth). The costs of raising Frank are a direct financial injury to the parents,
no different in immediate effect than the medical expenses resulting from the wrongful conception and birth
of a child. Government studies of the economic costs of
raising children provide a reasonable basis for judicial
assessment of the extent of this injury. (R.5) Therefore, Rebecca and Scott should recover for the costs of
rearing Frank.

Recovery for all emotional and pecuniary costs is necessary to compensate the Bell-Wesleys for the full extent of their injuries and to hold O'Toole liable for

7

the consequences of his negligence. This recovery is
not disproportionate to the actions of Dr. O'Toole; the
doctor could easily have limited his liability by taking
the simple step of providing proper post-operative care.
Full recovery by wrongful pregnancy claimants is necessary to deter sufficiently negligence in performing
vasectomies. Courts must assess doctors for the full
costs of their malfeasance in order to provide adequate
incentives for safe, effective medical procedures. See
Kingsbury v. Smith, 442 A.2d 1003, 1005 (N.H. 1982)
(stating that failure to recognize wrongful birth claims
would lower the standard of professional conduct and ex-
pertise in the area of family planning).

For Rebecca and Scott, the trial court's insistence
that the birth of a child is a blessing in all respects,
regardless of its parents' wishes, is meritless. Frank's
conception and birth substantially injured the Bell-
Wesleys' physical, emotional, and financial well-being.
Rebecca's pregnancy was accompanied by the severe emotional trauma that, after the birth of three deformed
children, the Bell-Wesleys had sought to avoid through
sterilization. Moreover, the couple's decision to undergo an irreversible sterilization operation demonstrated that they rejected procreation at any cost.
While they could have adopted children, Rebecca and
Scott instead chose to pursue a childless lifestyle, recognizing that parenthood entails numerous costs, burdens, and responsibilities that may outweigh its
attendant joys. Where a couple elects not to have children, it should be presumed that the birth of a child
does not benefit them. Cf. Hartke, 707 F.2d at 1552
(failed tubal ligation, resulting in birth of healthy

8

child, created wrongful birth claim against the physician); <u>Lovelace Medical Ctr. v. Mendez</u>, 805 P.2d 603,
612-13 (N.M. 1991) (holding that the birth of a healthy
child due to negligent sterilization can result in compensable damages). The Bell-Wesleys reassessed their
opportunities and resources and radically altered the
goals of their marriage. They decided to devote more
time to each other and to their careers, only to have
their expectations shattered as a result of O'Toole's
repeated negligence.

Policy considerations dictate that injuries to Scott
and Rebecca be compensated like those in any other medical malpractice action. Family planning decisions
should be within the exclusive province of those whom
the decisions will most affect -- children and their parents. Tens of millions employ contraceptives daily to
prevent the birth of children. These persons, by their
conduct, express the prevailing attitude of the community. <u>See generally</u> <u>Troppi v. Scarf</u>, 187 N.W.2d 511,
517 (Minn. Ct. App. 1971) (holding that negligent fill-
ing of a birth control prescription with tranquilizers
created a wrongful birth cause of action against the
pharmacist, with damages recoverable for pregnancy,
birth, and childrearing costs). Thus, the trial court's
declaration that a child's birth is always a blessing
does not reflect the manifest will of the people, the requirement for a judicial exception to standard tort law
doctrines. <u>Id.</u> at 516. Instead, it merely reflects the
paternalism of a bygone era.

Rebecca and Scott have also suffered the violation of
their constitutionally protected right to self-determina-

9

tion in the realm of family planning. The Bell-Wesleys'
determination that Scott would undergo a vasectomy was
an intimate, personal family planning matter that falls
within the zone of privacy and self-determination protected by the Constitution. See, e.g., Roe v. Wade, 410
U.S. 113, 152 (1973) (affirming that the Constitution
guarantees the right to privacy); Griswold v. Connecticut, 381 U.S. 479 (1965) (recognizing a constitutionally
protected zone of privacy in which married couples make
family planning decisions). Rebecca and Scott had a fundamental right to determine not to have children.
O'Toole's repeated negligence thwarted the exercise of
their right. When a doctor's negligence results in the
birth of an unwanted child, a substantial interference
with the fundamental rights of the parents occurs, and
the courts should recognize its significance. See Lovelace, 805 P.2d at 612-13 (stating that the harm in a
wrongful birth action is the invasion of the parents' legally protected interest in the financial security of
their family and the frustration of their desire to
limit the size of their family). Public policy prohib-
its immunizing negligent medical practitioners from tort
liability where to do so would have a negative impact on
the exercise of patients' constitutionally protected
rights. See Ochs, 445 A.2d at 885 ("[P]ublic policy cannot support an exception to tort liability when the
impact of such an exception would impair the exercise of
a constitutionally protected right.").

    Negligent physicians like Dr. O'Toole must not be al-
lowed to escape the consequences of their carelessness.
Faced with a blameworthy defendant, O'Toole, and his innocent victims, the Bell-Wesleys, this Court will not
serve society by granting immunity to the tortfeasor and

10

leaving his victims uncompensated. Public safety and basic fairness require that Dr. O'Toole pay for all the
consequences of his wrongful behavior. The Bell-Wesleys
should not be forced to absorb the costs of his
negligence.

Dr. O'Toole's negligence led to a birth which denied
Rebecca and Scott the opportunity to lead the lifestyle
they had chosen and imposed on them burdens they were entitled to avoid through sterilization. This claim does
not comment on the value of Frank Bell's life, because
Frank is not an item of damage in this suit. The issue
is not Frank or the love his parents feel for him, but
the negligence which had financial and emotional
repercussions on Scott and Rebecca's lives.

Recognition of the Bell-Wesleys' claim will not result in psychological harm to Frank if he discovers that
he was unplanned. Frank could easily be protected from
this unlikely event by keeping the names involved in
this action confidential. Most importantly, recovery by
the Bell-Wesleys will inure to Frank's emotional benefit, since it will relieve the economic pressure of raising an unexpected child and permit the parents to
concentrate on giving the child the love and care he
needs.

Rebecca and Scott Bell-Wesley have demonstrated all
of the elements that constitute medical malpractice and
are entitled to recover for the extensive injuries
caused by Dr. O'Toole's negligence. Any exception from
standard tort law would immunize O'Toole and victimize
Frank's innocent parents. An exception would also con-
travene public policies favoring family planning and
self-determination, discouraging careless behavior, and
promoting the redress of harms.

11

The argument that childrearing costs are too speculative can be discounted in light of other awards that the tort system and courts feel comfortable making, including those for pain and suffering and for wrongful death. Childrearing costs can be satisfactorily estimated using data available from the government and other sources. See Exhibit A, (R.5).

II.   IF THIS COURT WILL NOT AWARD FULL DAMAGES
      BECAUSE OF THE BENEFIT OF HAVING A CHILD, THIS
      COURT SHOULD APPLY THE BENEFIT RULE AND AWARD
      DAMAGES FOR THE COSTS OF RAISING FRANK BELL
      OFFSET BY THE BENEFIT OF HAVING HIM.

If this Court is unwilling to award full damages, Rebecca and Scott are at least entitled to the benefit rule, consistent with tort law's goals of deterrence and fair compensation for injuries. If the Court finds that having a healthy child is a benefit, then this should only lessen the total award for Scott and Rebecca rather than completely eviscerate it.

In situations in which courts will not award full damages, the most just compromise solution is the application of the benefit rule. The benefit rule requires the court to subtract the estimated benefit of the child to the parents from their recovery. See Burke v. Rivo, 551 N.E.2d 1, 5 (Mass. 1990). This approach is in conformity with the Restatement (Second) of Torts section 920, which states:

> When the defendant's tortious conduct has caused harm
> to the plaintiff or to his property and in so doing
> has conferred a special benefit to the interest of
> the plaintiff that was harmed, the value of the
> benefit conferred is considered in mitigation of
> damages, to the extent that this is equitable.

12

Restatement (Second) of Torts § 920 (1972). In another
failed vasectomy case, the Minnesota Supreme Court ruled
that a husband and wife were entitled to recovery for
the ,costs of raising an unwanted child, reduced by the
benefit of the child, after a doctor negligently performed the husband's vasectomy. Sherlock v. Stillwater
Clinic, 260 N.W.2d 169, 171 (Minn. 1977).

Similarly, the Massachusetts Supreme Judicial Court
ruled that a woman could recover for the costs of raising a healthy but unwanted child, offset by the estimated benefit of the child, after a doctor negligently
performed a sterilization procedure. Burke, 551 N.E.2d
at 6. While that court's ruling was limited to those
failed sterilizations that were originally obtained for
financial or economic reasons, the important social implications for the court's ruling also apply to situations in which a sterilization is obtained for eugenic
reasons and a family makes substantial financial decisions based on that judgment.

A ruling that the benefit of the child completely dis-
allows any recovery where a couple undergoes sterilization for eugenic reasons would improperly offset
emotional gain against financial loss. The emotional
benefits the Bell-Wesleys receive through the joys of
parenthood are of an entirely different nature and kind
than the financial injuries and the pain and suffering
inflicted on them by O'Toole's negligence. Rebecca and
Scott's deep love for Frank does not negate the fact
that his birth was neither planned nor desired. Their
affection for Frank will not provide the Bell-Wesleys
with the money to cover his expenses or replace the time

13

and energy diverted from their careers. Therefore, this Court should apply the benefit rule, in the event that it finds the birth of an unwanted child after a negligent sterilization a benefit.

CONCLUSION

Dr. O'Toole's repeated negligence caused the Bell-Wesleys substantial physical, financial, and emotional injuries that were left uncompensated by the Superior Court. Therefore, this Court should reverse the judgment of the Superior Court and Court of Appeals of the State of Ames and award full recovery to Rebecca and Scott Bell-Wesley.

Respectfully submitted,

Jane E. Harvey
Attorney for the Plaintiffs-Appellants

14

173

IN THE SUPREME COURT OF THE

STATE OF AMES

CIVIL ACTION NO. 96-2004

SCOTT AND REBECCA BELL-WESLEY, PLAINTIFFS-APPELLANTS

V.

DR. STEPHEN O'TOOLE, DEFENDANT-APPELLEE

BRIEF FOR THE DEFENDANT-APPELLEE

D. Nathan Neuville
Attorney for the Defendant-
   Appellee

Argument: December 14, 1996
Ames Courtroom
7:30 p.m.

TABLE OF CONTENTS

TABLE OF CITATIONS

CASES

ii

iii

QUESTIONS PRESENTED

Should the damages awarded to the parents of a child born after an unsuccessful vasectomy be limited to the costs associated with pregnancy, when the parents sought sterilization for eugenic reasons and the unexpected child is normal and healthy?

Should the "benefit rule" apply to a wrongful pregnancy suit, when the benefits of a child cannot be meaningfully compared to the costs?

Even if the "benefit rule" applies, do the child-rearing costs to wealthy parents who have always desired a child outweigh the intangible, life-long benefits of the child to the parents?

STATEMENT OF FACTS

Appellants Rebecca and Scott Bell-Wesley brought suit in the Superior Court of the State of Ames against Dr. Stephen O'Toole, an established Ames physician, seeking damages for the birth of a healthy, normal child following an unsuccessful sterilization. (R.1-4)

Mr. and Mrs. Bell-Wesley are a successful professional couple residing in Holmes, Ames. (R.1) Scott Bell-Wesley is an architect and Rebecca Bell-Wesley is an Assistant Attorney General for the State of Ames. (R.1) On three occasions before the January 1996 birth of their son, Frank Michael Bell, the Bell-Wesleys had attempted to start a family. (R.1) Each time, however, Mrs. Bell-Wesley gave birth to a congenitally deformed infant that died within six months. (R.1) Dr. O'Toole informed the Bell-Wesleys that there was a seventy-five percent chance that any child they conceived would suffer the same deformity. (R.1) For the sole purpose

1

of avoiding the conception of another deformed child, the Bell-Wesleys decided to have Dr. O'Toole sterilize Mr. Bell-Wesley. (R.7)

On October 16, 1993, Dr. O'Toole performed a vasectomy on Mr. Bell-Wesley. (R.1,11) After a follow-up sperm count, Dr. O'Toole mistakenly informed Mr. Bell-Wesley that he was sterile. (R.2) Eighteen months after the vasectomy, Mrs. Bell-Wesley discovered that she was pregnant. (R.2) On January 4, 1996, Mrs. Bell-Wesley gave birth to a healthy, normal son, Frank Michael Bell. (R.11-12) While they characterize Frank as an unwanted child, the Bell-Wesleys have declined to put him up for adoption. (R.12)

Although they profess great love for their son, the Bell-Wesleys brought suit against Dr. O'Toole, claiming to be injured by Frank's birth. (R.3) The Bell-Wesleys seek damages of approximately $566,000, including $150,000 for injury to their lifestyle and $250,000 for the financial and emotional costs of raising Frank. (R.3) Judge Nancy Llewenstein of the Superior Court found that the vasectomy was unsuccessful and that the sperm count was negligently performed. (R.11,12) The court awarded the Bell-Wesleys damages for the out-of-pocket costs, pain and suffering, and loss of consortium incident to the vasectomy. (R.13) The court refused to award damages for the costs of rearing Frank Bell, holding that the benefits to the Bell-Wesleys of this healthy, normal child outweighed the costs of raising him. (R.14) The Court of Appeals for the State of Ames affirmed. (R.18) The Bell-Wesleys appeal the lower courts' decisions.

2

STANDARD OF REVIEW

While this court may review issues of law de novo, it must defer to the trial court's findings of fact. <u>See</u> <u>Sherlock v. Stillwater Clinic</u>, 260 N.W.2d 169, 172 (Minn. 1977) (deferring to trial court determination of facts to support a negligence decision).

ARGUMENT

I.   THIS COURT SHOULD NOT AWARD THE BELL-WESLEYS DAMAGES FOR THE COSTS OF RAISING THEIR NORMAL, HEALTHY SON TO MAJORITY.

   A. <u>Frank's Birth Did Not Injure the Bell-Wesleys, Because They Sought Sterilization for Non-Economic Reasons</u>.

The damages awarded to the Bell-Wesleys should not include full child-rearing costs. The birth of a normal son to parents who procured a vasectomy solely to avoid having a deformed child should not be deemed an injury. <u>See</u> <u>Szekeres v. Robinson</u>, 715 P.2d 1076, 1077 (Nev. 1986) (finding no tort liability for wrongful pregnancy and awarding no damages). Even if the conception of the Bell-Wesleys' child was an injury, the birth of a healthy child was not. <u>See, e.g.</u>, <u>O'Toole v. Greenberg</u>, 477 N.E.2d 445 (N.Y. 1985); <u>Johnson v. Univ. Hosp. of Cleveland</u>, 540 N.E.2d 1370 (Ohio 1989). Many jurisdictions currently limit recovery in wrongful pregnancy cases to child-bearing costs. <u>See</u> Judy S. Loitherstein, <u>Towards Full Recovery - The Future of Damages Awards in Wrongful Pregnancy Cases</u>, 25 Suffolk U. L. Rev. 735 (1991). This Court should follow those jurisdictions.

3

The Bell-Wesleys have suffered no injury. For years they yearned for a healthy child like Frank. Before Frank's birth, the Bell-Wesleys had tried to start a family three times, only to see each attempt result in the birth of a deformed child who died in infancy. (R.1) The Bell-Wesleys abandoned their hopes of having a family only when Dr. O'Toole informed them that it was highly probable that any child they conceived would suffer the same deformity. Scott Bell-Wesley obtained a vasectomy solely to avoid the birth of another deformed child. (R.11)

The Bell-Wesleys escaped the injury they sought to avoid. Courts do not award full child-rearing costs where the parents, like the Bell-Wesleys, sought sterilization for eugenic (avoiding a genetic defect) or therapeutic (relating to health of the mother) reasons. See, e.g., Burke v. Rivo, 551 N.E.2d 1, 6 (Mass. 1990) (stating that where the purpose of sterilization was therapeutic, parents should not recover child-rearing costs). The Bell-Wesleys sought only to avoid the birth of a fourth deformed child; they cannot recover for the birth of the healthy, normal child they always wanted.

This rationale has persuaded courts to award damages for the pre-natal period only. In Hartke v. McKelway, 526 F. Supp. 97, 99 (D.D.C. 1981), aff'd. 707 F.2d 1544 (D.C. Cir. 1983), cert. denied 464 U.S. 983 (1983), for example, the plaintiff, Sandra Hartke, had suffered an ectopic pregnancy. Fearing that another pregnancy might be fatal, she obtained a tubal ligation. Id. Similarly, the Bell-Wesleys bore three children who died due to congenital deformities. Fearing the birth -- and

4

death -- of another child, they obtained sterilization.
(R.6) However, the sterilizations of both Mrs. Hartke
and Scott Bell-Wesley were unsuccessful. Furthermore,
the babies born to both were healthy. Id. at 99; (R.7).
Because Mrs. Hartke sought her sterilization for therapeutic reasons only, the court limited her damages to
the pre-natal period. Hartke, 526 F. Supp. at 105. The
Bell-Wesleys sought sterilization for the same reasons,
(R.6); their damages should also be limited.

   The Bell-Wesleys did not obtain a vasectomy for economic reasons. They did not decide they could not af-
ford a child or attempt to limit the size of their
family. Some courts have permitted recovery of child-
rearing costs where a child, born after a non-therapeu-
tic sterilization, creates the very situation the
parents sought to avoid: an economic drain on family resources or a simple increase in family size. See, e.g.,
Lovelace Medical Ctr. v. Mendez, 805 P.2d 603, 612-13
(N.M. 1991) (sterilization sought to limit family size);
Sherlock v. Stillwater Clinic, 260 N.W.2d 169 (Minn.
1977) (sterilization sought in order to limit family
size after birth of seventh child); Betancourt v. Gay-
lor, 344 A.2d 336, 339 (N.J. Super. 1975) (parents
sought to avoid expense of additional child). Scott and
Rebecca Bell-Wesley, however, decided upon sterilization
for purely therapeutic reasons. These two professionals
sought for years to expand their family and are fully capable of providing for their son. No court has ever permitted recovery of child-rearing costs under such
circumstances.

5

The Bell-Wesleys' constitutional privacy rights under Roe v. Wade, 410 U.S. 113 (1973), and Griswold v. Connecticut, 381 U.S. 479 (1965), are not at issue in this lawsuit. Roe and Griswold establish privacy rights that protect the Bell-Wesleys only against state action or government intrusion. See Roe, 410 U.S. at 153. There has been no state action against the Bell-Wesleys; Dr. O'Toole is a private individual, not a government agent. Roe and Griswold are also inapposite here because they articulate the right of parents to control their family's size. The Bell-Wesleys, however, were not seeking to control their family size; they procured Mr. Bell-Wesley's vasectomy for therapeutic reasons.

B. Awarding Full Child-Rearing Costs Harms the Mental Health of Unwanted Children, Discourages Doctors From Performing Needed Sterilizations, and Grants Windfalls to Parents.

Awarding full child-rearing costs might cause Frank severe emotional trauma. When a child such as Frank learns that he was unwanted, that his parents felt injured by his birth, and that they were unwilling to pay for his expenses themselves, he will suffer serious emotional injury. Society does not so readily dismiss the emotional trauma of a child. See, e.g., Wilbur v. Kerr, 628 S.W.2d 568, 571 (Ark. 1982) (denying recovery for the expense of raising an unwanted, healthy child).

The deterrence goal of negligence is not served by awarding the costs of raising the child. The recovery the Bell-Wesleys seek is grossly out of proportion with Dr. O'Toole's culpability. See

6

Johnson v. Univ. Hosp. of Cleveland, 540 N.E.2d 1370
(Ohio 1989) (adopting limited damages rule in wrongful
pregnancy suit on public policy grounds); Rieck v. Medical Protective Co., 219 N.W.2d 242, 244-45 (Wis. 1974)
(precluding recovery for birth of unwanted child because
of the excessive burden on physicians and other public
policy concerns). The costs of raising Frank to adulthood, estimated by the Bell-Wesleys at over $250,000,
(R.3), are astronomical in comparison to those involved
in a vasectomy, a low-cost operation performed in the
doctor's own office. The goal of deterrence has already
been adequately served by the Superior Court's award of
damages for the pre-natal period and, more importantly,
by the accompanying injury to Dr. O'Toole's professional
reputation. Furthermore, the costs of raising a child
are speculative and any damages based on them would be
impossible to determine accurately. See Hitzemann v.
Adam, 18 N.W.2d 102 (Neb. 1994) (refusing to award child-
rearing costs in wrongful pregnancy case in part because
costs are difficult to assess).

To go beyond the trial court's award and assess liability grossly out of proportion with Dr. O'Toole's negligence would result in the practice of defensive
medicine and in increased sterilization costs. Faced by
the prospect of devastatingly disproportionate liability
and dramatically increased insurance costs, physicians
may counsel against sterilization when the operation is
in their patient's best interest. Physicians will pass
their increased costs on to their patients by charging
greater fees for sterilization, denying a socially valuable family planning option to low-income patients.

7

Because the Bell-Wesleys did not procure sterilization for financial reasons, allowing them to recover the
costs of raising Frank would grant them a windfall. See
Hartke v. McKelway, 707 F.2d 1544, 1553-55 (D.C. Cir.
1983), cert. denied, 464 U.S. 983 (1983); Rieck, 219
N.W.2d at 244-45. The Bell-Wesleys will enjoy every
benefit, tangible and intangible, associated with
raising a healthy child. Meanwhile, Dr. O'Toole and,
via insurance, the rest of society, will be forced to
bear all of the costs intertwined with these benefits.
The Bell-Wesleys never sought to avoid these costs and
are fully capable of bearing them.

Awarding child-rearing costs to the Bell-Wesleys
would threaten the emotional well-being of children,
have deleterious effects upon family structure, and
impose excessive liability upon physicians. It might
be more palatable to attempt to ignore these concerns
where the wrongful pregnancy claimants could not provide
for their child's needs or where the child was
unhealthy. The Bell-Wesleys, however, are financially
capable of raising a child and have become the parents
of the healthy child they desired.

II.   THE "BENEFIT RULE" SHOULD NOT BE ADOPTED BY
      THIS COURT, BECAUSE THE BENEFITS OF A CHILD
      CANNOT BE QUANTIFIED.

The use of the "benefit rule" is inappropriate in
wrongful pregnancy suits, because the benefits received
cannot be weighed against the costs of raising the
child. The "benefit rule" should not be applied here.
Several jurisdictions have turned to the "benefit rule"

8

to offset awards of child-rearing damages. <u>See, e.g.</u>,
<u>Ochs v. Borelli</u>, 445 A.2d 883 (Conn. 1982). The
prospect of using the "benefit rule" to offset damages
should not influence the decision whether or not to
limit damages to the pre-natal period. The child-
rearing costs should not be awarded and the "benefit
rule" should not be applied.

The "benefit rule" should not be applied in this
case, because the benefit of Frank Michael Bell to his
parents cannot be monetized. The "benefit rule" of the
Restatement (Second) of Torts provides:

> When the defendant's tortious conduct has caused harm
> to the plaintiff or to his property and in so doing
> has conferred a special benefit to the interest of
> the plaintiff that was harmed, the value of the
> benefit conferred is considered in mitigation of
> damages, to the extent that it is equitable.

Restatement (Second) of Torts § 920 (1972). Under this
rule, the "harm" to parents alleging wrongful pregnancy
and seeking full child-rearing costs is the financial
suffering, while the "benefit" is the lifelong relationship with a child. Because this benefit is not
quantifiable, the two cannot be compared. <u>See</u> <u>Johnson</u>
<u>v. Univ. Hosp. of Cleveland</u>, 540 N.E.2d 1370 (Ohio
1989). While the benefits of a child are great, they
are also largely intangible and elude financial calculation. To place a dollar value upon these benefits would
be to denigrate the value of the child's life. Many
courts have recognized that these benefits cannot and
should not be subject to judicial assessment; they have
concluded that the incalculable benefits received by the
parents outweigh the costs of raising a healthy child as

9

a matter of law. <u>See</u> <u>Beardsley v. Wierdsma</u>, 650 P.2d
288, 293 (Wyo. 1982) (noting that any attempt to measure
these benefits would be a misplaced attempt to put a specific dollar value on a child's life); <u>see also</u> <u>Cockrum
v. Baumgartner</u>, 447 N.E.2d 385, 388-89 (Ill. 1983); <u>Ter-
rell v. Garcia</u>, 496 S.W.2d 124, 128 (Tex. Ct. App.
1973), <u>cert. denied</u>, 415 U.S. 927 (1974).

III. EVEN IF THE "BENEFIT RULE" APPLIES, THE
      EMOTIONAL BENEFITS THE BELL-WESLEYS WILL
      RECEIVE FROM FRANK MICHAEL BELL OUTWEIGH
      THEIR FINANCIAL COSTS.

The Bell-Wesleys' demonstrated desire for a healthy
child requires a holding that the benefits predominate
in this case, even if this Court adopts the "benefit
rule." When the Bell-Wesleys conceived each of their
three deceased children, they had determined that the
joys of parenthood exceeded the emotional and financial
costs of pregnancy, birth, and child-rearing. Nothing
indicates that the Bell-Wesleys ever altered their evaluation; they sought sterilization solely because they
feared the birth of a fourth deformed child. (R.8) The
purpose for which the parents sought sterilization is
the most telling evidence of whether, on balance, the
child's birth actually damaged the couple. <u>See</u> <u>Univer-
sity of Arizona Health Services Ctr. v. Superior Court
of Maricopa County</u>, 667 P.2d 1294, 1300 (Ariz. 1983).
Because the Bell-Wesleys' purpose was to avoid a
deformed child, the birth of their normal son has not
damaged them.

10

The Bell-Wesleys' own evaluation of the costs and benefits of parenthood, evident from their repeated attempts to have a healthy child, demonstrates that Frank's birth was, on balance, a benefit to them. Any further damage award would unjustly enrich the Bell-Wesleys at Dr. O'Toole's and society's expense.

Frank's birth will bring his parents all the joy and satisfaction normally associated with parenthood. The equitable principle embodied in the "benefit rule" requires that the Bell-Wesleys' damages be offset by the value of the child's aid, comfort, and society which will benefit the parents for the duration of their lives. Sherlock v. Stillwater Clinic, 260 N.W.2d 169, 176 (Minn. 1977). The Bell-Wesleys' subsequent behavior indicates that they do not feel injured by Frank's existence. They have declined to place Frank up for adoption. (R.8) This demonstrates they acknowledge that they will receive a benefit. See Public Health Trust v. Brown, 388 So. 2d 1084, 1086 (Fla. App. 1980) (noting that the failure to place the child up for adoption indicates that the parents are benefited by keeping the child).

Moreover, they have not altered their lifestyle greatly since Scott Bell-Wesley's vasectomy. The only visible change in the Bell-Wesleys' circumstances is Rebecca's new position in the Attorney General's office. Mrs. Bell-Wesley had held this job for less than eighteen months when she discovered she was pregnant. Her affection for Frank demonstrates that she did not become so caught up in her new position during this short period that she abandoned her desire for a child.

11

This couple desperately wished to have a healthy child of their own. Thus, Frank's arrival was a long hoped-for blessing.

Child-rearing will place a relatively slight burden upon the Bell-Wesleys. As an architect and a lawyer respectively, Mr. and Mrs. Bell-Wesley will have no difficulty supporting Frank financially. The Bell-Wesleys have no other children, so Frank's birth will not deprive any siblings of parental care or support. For years the couple has been fully prepared to accept the economic and emotional costs of raising a child, yet the list of damages that they now claim is no more than a catalogue of the costs normally associated with bearing and raising a child. The Bell-Wesleys' own assessment of parenthood establishes that the benefits of Frank's birth outweigh these costs. Frank's presence actually benefits the interests the Bell-Wesleys claim were harmed. While they allege injury to their childless lifestyle, their persistent attempts at childbearing demonstrate that Frank enhances their lifestyle. Frank will even provide future financial benefits because a child is some security for the parents' old age. Terrell v. Garcia, 496 S.W.2d 124, 128 (Tex. Ct. App. 1973), cert. denied, 415 U.S. 927 (1974). Failure to offset the benefits of Frank's birth based on a same interest rationale will unjustly enrich the Bell-Wesleys, producing a result antithetical to the "benefit rule."

12

CONCLUSION

For the foregoing reasons, the judgments of the Superior Court and the Court of Appeals should be affirmed.

Respectfully submitted,

D. Nathan Neuville
Attorney for the Defendant-Appellee

INDEX

References are to Pages

INDEX

References are to Pages

INDEX

References are to Pages

INDEX

References are to Pages